JPP PUBLISHING/PRINTING

On October 14, 1966, his Holiness Pope Paul VI confirmed the decree of the Sacred Congregation for the propagation of the Faith, under number 58/16 (A.A.S.), permitting the publication of writings about supernatural apparitions, even if they do not have a "nihil obstat" from ecclesiastical authorities.

THE SACRED HEART...AN ABYSS OF LOVE AND PAIN
First Edition
© Invitation to Love Jesus 1995

Jesus gave the following Message about the First edition of The Sacred Heart - An Abyss of Love and Pain:
"...I am pleased with the Book of My Words and I thank all who loved Me enough to produce it. I Love you. I tell you that it will hit this world like an explosion. Ready yourselves for it. I Love you." Thursday 21 December 1995

Second Edition
© Invitation to Love Jesus 2005
ISBN: 1-904495-20-6

Distribution of and further information about the Messages of Love as given by Jesus through the two Patricks can be obtained from:

AN INVITATION TO LOVE JESUS
Sacred Heart House of Prayer
46 James Street
Cookstown
Co. Tyrone
Northern Ireland
BT80 8LT
Tel: 028867 66377   Fax: 028867 62247
info@thetwopatricks.org

CONTENTS

CONTENTS

FOREWORD

I recommend the pages which follow for many reasons. First is the overwhelming attention to the Sacred Heart of Jesus. This is welcome to many who were brought up, as I was, in a spirit of veneration and total confidence in this revelation of the mystery of Christ - we were personally consecrated to the Heart of Jesus or, as was the case with me, we belonged to a family which had been so-consecrated by a priest.

With reflection, we could enter more profoundly into the sublime mystery. We could follow the phases of its unfolding through the Christian centuries. A landmark was the revelation to Saint Margaret Mary Alacoque: "Behold this Heart which has so loved men..." But the idea which had meant so much to Catholics, which had been an inspiration to heroic souls in every walk of life, seemed latterly, in the secularising climate of our time, to suffer from the strange opposition which has arisen against important, cherished Catholic ideals.

Signs of renewal are fortunately evident, and here is one which I warmly welcome. It is expressed in language which is encouraging and consoling. The direct, personal style should make it not only very readable, but accessible. There is much else to ponder in the text and I am sure that many will find spiritual motivation, conversion perhaps - if not from waywardness, from a lukewarm piety, or casual attitude to their religion. The centre, the attractive power is none other than Jesus Christ, the 'Way, the Truth and the Life.' The ultimate goal of all Christian endeavour must be intimacy with Him. May the reader of these pages find help in this wonderful undertaking in Words which are so deeply moving.

Fr. Michael O'Carroll, C.S.Sp. (RIP)
Feast of Our Lady's Nativity,
8 September 1995

INTRODUCTION

"Behold, I stand at the door of your heart knocking, ever knocking."

Have our hearts become so hardened that we cannot hear His knock? The great creating Father formed these hearts of ours to be home for His tremendous Love. He created, in each of us, a still, inner temple where God Himself could dwell - a peaceful sanctuary which would radiate His Love to the world. He waits for us to answer His patient knocking.

"Come into My Arms, so that you can feel My Loving and tender embrace." His Invitation is for all. His Love is immeasurable - His Heart a Universe of Tenderness. His is an all-consuming Love; an eternal, infinite, undying Love; an unfathomable, inexhaustible, erupting Love that longs to pour its rivers of Love into the thirsty hearts of mankind. This Divine Heart is a reservoir of burning Love. It contains only Love, and yet it is met by so much unlove.

Weary of our sinning, pained by our neglect, He waits hour by hour, day by day, year by year, in the Tabernacles of our world, silently offering, to the Father, the little love that we give in our efforts to appease the Agony of His great, fiery Heart. Our little means so much to Him. Jesus Loves us even unto folly.

This sin-sick world needs to learn again the forgiving, compassionate Love of our God. In the following Messages, this Triune God offers us an amnesty of pardon and compassion. Let us come to the outstretched Arms of Jesus, lean our heads on His Breast, and hear the beating of the Heart of the Man-God. This Heart longs to uplift us, to Forgive and strengthen us, to make us whole and to empower us to live in His Love. We can immerse our selfishness and sin in the measureless ocean of His Mercy. The Heart of Jesus is truly an Abyss of Love Divine.

Sr. Monica Cavanagh, P.B.V.M.
Feast of Our Lady of Sorrows,
15 September 1995

PREFACE

The Most Sacred Heart of Jesus has, in His Wisdom, dictated these Words to the whole world. This communication is unique, as it spells out many things that have been long-suffered by Jesus at the hands of us, His created.

Many times He speaks in extreme Pain; the kind of Pain that we have never taken into consideration when thinking of Him, or meditating upon His Passion. Jesus expresses much of that Pain and Love in these Words.

The 'Abyss' that Jesus speaks of, is the Great Vessel of His Heart, that tenderly Loves us 'even to folly.' He is endeavouring, so passionately, to convey the secrets of His Heart. His Treasures are contained here, but He emphasises that all the languages of this world could not describe these Treasures. He tells us that we do not know these things because we have never taken the time to find out. As He speaks the Words Himself: *"...My lambs, you never took the time to find out."*

Jesus speaks about sin. He tells us that *"...the smallest sin that is committed is like spitting in My Face. Do you know that the greatest sin is like Me being tied and gagged and thrown into a furnace? I have no way of defending Myself..."* Need any more be said of this?

This passionate God stoops to our level and asks us to simply look at the truth, His Truth, to see the many lies that we tell ourselves. He complains that *"...you blame Me...for the many disasters and much suffering that is wrought by mankind. It is simple. It is wealth and power that you seek, not Love. You hold My children in bondage in your lust and your greed."*

For the first time in these Messages of Love, Jesus speaks as the Triune God. He sheds much Divine Light upon the inherent Mystery of the Trinitarian God, *"...the Godhead..."*, *"...a Constant Love..."* He tells us that Forgiveness is the Trinity's Way of bringing Light into a place of darkness. This is expressed in the silent statement of the Crucifixion - the ultimate Sacrifice expounding this Forgiveness in its totality.

This book is for the whole world. It is a statement that makes us intimate with our God. Reading this book and marvelling at the beauty of its Words can only render them dead and of no consequence. They must be lived.

The Two Patricks
Feast of the Most Sacred Heart of Jesus,
23 June 1995

THE SACRED HEART...

AN ABYSS
OF
LOVE AND PAIN

AS GIVEN BY JESUS TO THE TWO PATRICKS
SECOND EDITION

CHAPTER 1

THE TRUTH

My children of this world, I, the Lord your God, address you. I come in this way, as I have come many times throughout history, to tell you of the things of Heaven. In this time, I reveal to this world the great Pain that is in Me. I do this, My little ones, to show you both My Pain and My Love.

Many of you, My children, do not believe that your God could be in Pain in this way, but here I am to tell you of it.

This is a weary God who would speak with you, a God weary of the sin and blasphemy and unlove that this world offers as a sacrifice to Him. I tell you, creation, of My Pain so that you can look at Me through the reality as it is and not as you think that it should be.

I give this world, once again, this Heart that is all Love and I give it simply in these Words. They are Words that you have heard before many times and in many ways, for they cannot change. I remain the same, yesterday, today and tomorrow. I give you now the Pain that is endured by Me in your name and for your sake.

My little ones, you will not see the reality of your ways and the lies that you tell yourselves that you serve Me, but all the time you are like the Pharisees. So I take this Heart, once again, and I try to give it to the world. I give it in Love, Forgiveness and in much Pain. I am willing to Suffer again for you if it were not to be in vain. Ah, little ones, I would Suffer again even if it were in vain.

I wish to give these Words to the world as Drops of Blood from My Sacred Heart, so that they might see it for what it is; an Abyss of Eternal, Fiery Love that is never put out. To show that, in order to burn unquenched, it must suffer great Pain for so little. For men still offer Me their ungrateful love. It is a love that does not long for Heavenly things but only temporal.

This Heart I give in its entirety and it shines like many suns. It casts much Light on mankind but, through the darkness of sin, he has created so many clouds that it is not allowed to penetrate.

Ah, the Treasure that so few behold in its goodness. The Graces that are lost through indifference to Me. My children, so much Pain, for so little.

This Love that is in Me bursts like so many seeds within the earth as I watched creation take its first steps into the Light; for Light I created upon this earth. I did not create darkness.

See these Words, if you have not seen and refuse to listen to the many others that fall from this Heart, so filled with scars and gashes, but still they come with My Love.

Even now, as I speak these Words, the burden that weighs upon Me presses Me to the ground as I fell with the weight of sins beneath the Cross that I carried for you. Do you think, My children, that your God cannot cry out in His Agony? Do you think that I can carry this load indefinitely? Children, children, these Words I speak in human terms for you could not understand the Truth. Look how I shield you from the Truth of My Suffering, even now, when the Pain is great.

Do you wish to know, children, or will you put these Words aside to gather dust, as you have done with many others that I have given to you? Where are you, My children, where are you that I have given My Body, Blood, Soul and Divinity for? Are you lost? Then come, follow the drips of Blood that you see, for I lose much Blood in My Pain. I await for you to come to Me in My prison of the Blessed Sacrament, and the walls are cold and lifeless, for there is no joy when there is no one there.

The greatest insults are yet to come. The churches are now being closed, and in many I have not only been abandoned behind locked doors, but the church doors are also locked and barred. These are insults to Me. How many of you sit in your homes with your televisions and do not have time to visit Me?

Ah, My children, so much Pain, so much ingratitude, so much indifference. Look at Me in My Passion as I stood before Pilate. I remained silent for I knew that I would Die. My only thoughts were you.

O, children, this Heart is on its Knees in begging you to return; to return to Love. So much Pain from a people that say that they love Me. I can see what is in your hearts, My little ones; I can see the truth of what you offer to Me and this is My Pain. I wish to be with you, not shut away from you. I wish to Love you within your soul. Why do you run away from Me with so many other things? Where is your treasure? Does it lie within the things of this earth that perish? The things that are like the grass of the field, that are here today and gone tomorrow?

In these Words, I cry out to this world for mercy. Yes, My children, mercy. My Heart is an Ocean of Mercy, yet the mercy that is given upon this earth from one to another of My children is little. Give your brothers and sisters mercy, and you give it to Me. Can you hear the pleas as these Words touch you? Or do you ignore them even as they are spoken to you?

Love, My children, was carried in the Womb of the Virgin, My Mother, as was foretold in Scripture. It was born into this world, into human ways. A God, truly among His people, and yet they do not wish to see.

I tell you now that this Heart stands before you in these Words of Great Pain. It causes Me Pain to give you these Words, for they tear at already opened Flesh, so that I stand before you as just a Carcass of

Flesh and Bones. Can you take the Truth, little ones? Or do you not wish to know this Pain of Mine? Do you see why I must speak these Words of Pain? Or do you already turn your head away?

Here is this Love; here is the Pain; it is before you in this Heart. These Words are My Heart. They are not idle Words, nor are they lies. They are the very Truth that I am, and they are the Way and the Life. Yes, it is Me, the Lord, your God, who speaks with you. I speak of Pain, great Pain, that you take for granted in your worldly living. I am weary, children, I am so weary of the Pain that is in Me.

CHAPTER 2

LIVING PAIN

My people, do you really understand My Love? Look at My Cross. See its Love; cherish it with your hearts. See the Truth of what it really is. My Cross is a personal symbol of Love to each one of you. I Died for you, My child, on this instrument of torture. I saw you as you were in your mother's womb and I watched you grow. I Loved you. I watched your birth. I saw every moment of your life as you grew - every fall, every stumble, every time that you would deny Me and your brother. I took all of this onto Myself so that you could have Eternal Life. Have you not realised what I have done for you? Can you not see how easy it is to enter My Father's Kingdom? I did it all for you, but you will not listen. You will not come.

O, My children, My children, will you not come? Please, please, please come to Me. Do not deny Me any longer. I Died for you so that you could be with Me. This day, I, your God, your Jesus, kneel before you, My child. Yes, it is you, My little one, whom I speak to as you read these Words of pure Love. I ask a little favour of you. Would you take one last look at My Passion and see it as it really is? Take your life and place it there. For in Truth I tell you, this is what you should have suffered to be cleansed of all your sin, so that you could enter Heaven.

For no mark or blemish of sin can go there. It is a place of pure Light, pure Love. Look, My little one, as I Suffered in Gethsemane. It was when I saw your sin, and all the sins of your brothers and sisters, who had lived and who would live upon this earth - I knew that I would have to take all of these and suffer for them to have you with Me.

I did not want to lose one of you; no, not one. My Burden was great as I fell to the ground with the weight of sin. My Humanness could not take it. Blood was forced from Me, as you would sweat, My little one. I was totally alone. My friends had fallen asleep at the gate; but I would not give up this Burden, for I Loved you so much. O, My little child, how can I convince you of My Love? Please, do not turn Me away.

As I lay there, I heard the sound of a group of men coming towards the Garden. I knew that My time had come. They came and bound Me and I was taken to My accusers. Behold! The Son of Man led away like a common criminal. Although My Pain was great, the Love and joy to know that you would be with Me was greater. But alas, My Burden grew more intense when I saw how many of My children would not accept what I have done for them. How many would reject My Love and turn away from Me!

Oh, My children, My children, why will you not listen? Why will you not come? Have I done all in vain?

See, My children, as I stood before Pilate, I took your place. This is why I kept silent. I knew I had to take your burden, your punishment, so that you could be with Me.

They kicked Me, they punched Me. They tore off My clothes and tied Me to a pillar. When the whip purged My Flesh, it was pierced for you and all your brothers and sisters, who have lived and would live upon this earth. Each lash I felt billions of times. Each kick, each thump, each insult, each mockery as they insulted your Friend, your God - I felt all of these billions of times.

Look, My little ones, now see all My Passion as it really was - not the way that you think, for this is the Truth that I speak in these Words. Now can you place yourself, and all My little ones, in the rest of My Suffering? Now can you see why I have said: "Love one another...", for it is I, Jesus, that you love in your brother and sister. No matter who they are or what they have done. I live in all men. I Forgive all as I Forgive you.

CHAPTER 3

THE DISUSED HEART

Little children, when I created your hearts, I not only created an organ to keep you alive, but I also created an innerness in which I could dwell. Just like the working parts of the outer heart, the inner was created to the specific working order of Love. It was to be an inner factory, in which I could work and produce much Love, that would be given free of charge.

It was created so that Living Streams of Love could pour from the reservoir of My own Heart, through pumping into your own hearts, and out into the world. This was My creation, this was My Dream.

Very few hearts are used in this way. There is no lofty path needed for this to happen. The key is simply to love.

I look into hearts and they cause Me Pain, for many are in darkness. I find no love within them, but hardened stone, so that no love can enter them - far from the gratitude that I asked for from men, far from the return of Love. The doors are shut fast and refuse to open. Hearts that are fully opened know the freedom that only I can give.

My children, My Love is an Erupting Love; a Tap of Great Love. It has no depth. It knows no bounds. It is a jealous Love. It Loves all mankind and cannot help itself in its folly of Loving them - a Universe of Tenderness that overflows Great Pain, for My Love and My Pain are One. They are inseparable. This Love cannot Love without Pain. When it sees the many disused hearts that could know Love, but refuse it in favour of darkness, Blood seeps from Me and I cry out to the world of a Love that is tortured and beaten by man's complacency. I relive, many times, this Suffering and I am Scourged again and again.

Ah, My infants, My babes, I Love you. I cry out many Words of Love and many Tears as I stand before the doors of your hearts knocking, ever knocking. There is no reply. You, who read these Words, can you feel the Pain and Sorrow that is in Me? See a Heart of Great Love that is immersed in Suffering with no relief.

Ah, My little ones, there are not the Words within all the languages of this world that would describe the Pain and the Love that is within Me. If you, who read this, could even begin to understand, you would remain silent for many years, for you could not utter a single sigh in keeping with the Love that is Mine.

Many times, all Heaven has stood silent in the wake of the great Pain and Suffering that overcomes Me. It is an all-consuming Love-Pain that tears. It is as though I were driven with many, many thorns that twist and turn in every direction and these fed on the sap of sin, ingratitude, complacency and, as each is committed, they grow and each plunge through Me and every part of Me. My Heart is pierced with many swords, for it is My Heart that feels most of the Pain. It is a Heart built of Love - its Walls are Love, its energy is Love; every beat is Love. Its only thought is Love, its action is Love and its reward is Pain. For Pain is the currency with which man pays Me. If it were anything else, it would be a return of love, not ingratitude.

If souls would take the time to call Me, to know Me, to spend time with Me, then they would be filled with Love. For this Heart cannot refuse a heart that is used for love.

Already, as I dictate these Words, I can feel the disbelief that is in many of you; "God does not suffer Pain anymore," is your cry. Do you not know, My children, do you not know? That on My Cross of Love I inherited your sufferings? How could I feel anything else? Look at your relationship with Me. How many times do you sit before Me in My Tabernacle-Prison and simply love Me for all those who do not love Me? How many times do you walk by without even a glance? Oh, children, children, children, do you not know that, if you would turn to Me, I would shower you in Mercy, in Love? Do you not know that I am always here, ready to set aside My own Pain and welcome you into My Arms?

Oh, My little ones, why do you make Me despair of you? If I were to allow you to see Me in My Pain, your minds would be tormented forever by just one image of Me in this way.

You see, children? This Pain of Mine is still the Suffering of the Cross. I still Suffer, because all do not accept My Salvation, which shines like many Lights and has, in some way, touched each person in this world. Until all accept, it must be this way. You, My children of this world, could help by seeing My Way, My Truth and My Life for what it is and living it. Then others would see it and come to know Me. But if you continue in your own truth, then My Pain will continue.

Do you know, My children, that the smallest sin that is committed is like spitting in My Face? Do you know that the greatest sin is like Me being tied and gagged and thrown into a furnace? I have no way of defending Myself.

These are things that you did not know because, My lambs, you never took the time to find out. In your time spent with Me you only ask Me for your needs, you do not take time to listen to My Words that are within you. When you receive Me in My Eucharist, you do not realise that I am within you. I wish to move from My Tabernacle-Prison into a soul that knows My Spirit of joy and freedom. But instead, I move into another prison, where there is none of these things, for I am soon forgotten.

There are many things that you do not take time to understand, My children, yet you say that you love Me.

CHAPTER 4

PRISON OF PAIN

See! Look! Behold! I am your God. I am your Saviour. See Me in your midst in the Tabernacles of this world. These cold, grey walls that surround Me penetrate this Heart with much Pain. Ah! The Pain would not seem so bad if there was the joy of seeing you come to Me.

Where are you?

When I look from this prison of Mine and I see empty churches - this is raw Pain. It scourges Me. It tears this Heart to think that you know that I am here and you do not come. It was for you that I made it possible that I would spend lifetimes here in this prison. Do you understand that it was I who had to accept the Pain of these walls even knowing that you would not come?

Ah, child, look into these Eyes. Look to their depth and see My Love. Look behind the Love and you will find the Pain that I speak of. My children do not look to the depths of Me. They do not wish to see. They are the blind leading the blind.

I travel the dark path of Pain, the Pain that all My children feel. Its darkness penetrates and twists; it tears at My Heart like so many daggers. It is never-ending. It is an abyss and there is no way out for Me. I am kept as a Prisoner in it and you will not set Me free by your love.

These multitude of nights that I have kept vigil in My loneliness for you. It is a waiting game in this prison. There are very few who will come to Me. If you really loved Me, children, you would run to Me at every opportunity. You would not hesitate to do anything else but run to this open Heart - step inside its many, many Wounds. Myriads of paths lead to the deepest centre, where I await you, to give you the treasures that I have told you of. You will see, know and feel its great Pain if you wish.

Do you know what it is like in this prison wilderness that I am in? Do you know the Pain that is in Me? Many of My little ones say that they cannot communicate with Me because I am far away from them. But no, I am here. They cannot see because they do not believe. They have deliberately removed themselves from Me and gone towards the things of this earth. I am present here with you; I have not left you orphans.

How can I convince you of the Pain and the Love? This great Sacrifice is for you and you alone. Talk with Me and spend time in doing so.

Come and tell Me your fears, all these I am, for I was totally human and I know these things.

Second upon second, minute upon minute, hour upon hour, day upon day, week upon week, month upon month, year upon year - this is My Life as I await, My children... and each day is like a thousand years to Me - all because I wait for you to come to Me in My Prison of Pain. By your visit to Me, it is like a few drops of water to slake this great thirst of Mine. So very few precious drips come My way.

As you read these Words that I speak with you now, does your heart not bleed with tenderness and love for Me, as you realise these things that I tell you? These Words are pure Words of communication of a Creator to His created. They are Words of undying Love, given to you to call you to the Salvation that is already prepared, bought and Lovingly given, free of charge. It is the Water of Living Life that I give to you.

Let these Words penetrate your little hearts, for a shaft of Divine Light penetrates your darkness in these Words of Pain that I give you. A ray of My inexhaustible Love touches you in these Words. Let these Words dance with joy in your heart, as I pierce you with this Love-Pain. Does your heart not burn at the passion that I express in these Words of pure Love? Let Me be your Food, for I am the Living Bread which has come down from Heaven to live in you and through you and with you, in all intimacy, tenderness and Love.

Ah, My children, a great sadness has overtaken Me as I dictate these Words. I ask you, will these too be in vain? Will they be read in a little while and then discarded? Many Words of Mine gather dust within your hearts. This is the sadness of this Heart. This is the Pain; this is the Love. I say that I Love you; I say that I want you with Me.

I say all these things to you to what avail, My little ones? To what avail? Are they Words of a great folly of a God who is Love? If this is the case then they are blown by every wind that is on this earth, lost and forgotten. They are dead if you do not make them live.

Let Me live; let Me live in you, as once I dreamed that I would live in all men through My Sacrifice on the Cross of Love. Are you with Me fully, or are you against Me?

CHAPTER 5

SACRIFICE IN UNION

My children, for many years I have asked you for sacrifices through My Saints and My Mother. But alas, My little ones, you still do not understand the good of sacrifice. Do you not realise that when you offer sacrifices to Me, that you are united with Me upon My Cross of Love? This is love, when you give of yourself; this is dying to yourself. As I gave everything of Myself upon the Cross for you, in offering sacrifice, this is walking in My Footsteps and We are united and become One.

Do not look to what your brother or your sister offers; all that I want is what you offer. Little and great, these are all equally important in My Eyes. Do not think that I would refuse anything that is offered to Me, as long as it is offered in humility and love, for all of this is important in the Salvation of this world. My children, I have asked for prayer, fasting and sacrifice, but all of these can be offered as small and great sacrifices.

I understand that many times you do not feel that you can be bothered coming to Me in prayer, or you feel that you cannot find the time. Is it not a sacrifice to go totally against your feelings? To simply come and find time, even if you come and sit with Me in the silence of your room and say nothing, you are with Me. Yes, My children, to simply sit with Me; I enjoy your company, for I Myself sit with you, holding you and Loving you, My precious child. Do not be concerned if you cannot feel Me, but simply believe that I am with you, filling your heart with My Love.

Fasting, children, is another form of sacrifice which can be offered in many ways. Do not look to the greater ways until you have discovered the smaller, My children, as My Mother has told you. Begin by offering little sacrifices and in time these will build into greater ones. Simply by abstaining from a glass of water or a piece of bread for one hour - this, My children, I receive with great joy, for you have shown your love for Me by giving of yourself. All is sacrifice, prayer, fasting and abstaining from the ways of the world. Sacrifice can be offering Me a little time from books, music, night life, cigarettes or hobbies. I do not ask you to give these up, but for a little of them, and then My burden is lightened by your caring and your sacrifice. Simply going against yourself causes pain, which is My Pain that you carry for love of Me, your God. My children, I will not ask these things of you, but I simply ask that you consider. I Love you, children, with an Everlasting Love. Oh, child, how I Love all of you and desire that you be with

Me in My Father's Kingdom.

CHAPTER 6

MY CHURCH, MY BODY

Oh, My little ones, if only My Dream were dreamed, then I could rest a little before I begin this eternity of Suffering for all of My little ones who came to be lost. Their memories shall be engraved upon this Heart forever. On every Cell and Ventricle they shall be forever remembered. Through the Pain of Love, I shall Suffer their loss.

I speak, My lambs, of My Church, My Body. This Dream, behold it. Behold the Dream of a God to live upon this earth with His people. A Dream that was to be dreamed forever.

Look, My Church, My Body, I am calling out to you in these few simple Words of Love. I am calling you to return. Return to the Ways of your God. I gave simple Words while I was upon this earth, so that all of you, who rule My Church, could live the simple life of servants. Where is your service? Is it caught in the web of earthly things? Look, My priests and My daughters and My sons, look to the Ways of your God and let the spiritual things that you know of Me permeate through to My sheep - not the ways that you have learned from the ways of this world.

Have I not raised Prophets from every generation? Have I not revealed to you My Words again and again and again so that you could see My Way? Have these Words not been like a lamp to your feet? I ask you, My Church, My Body; are you like the Pharisees, the Saducees, who were the embodiment of My Law, but yet they did not recognise Me?

Would you recognise Me if I came before you now? Have you individually walked your own separate ways? So many questions that I wish to be answered, but yet so many of you are blind. How can the blind lead the blind?

Ah, My little ones, do not drive My lambs, but lead them in simplicity and love. Begin to realise that, for all your earthly strivings, you cannot add one cubit to the spiritual lives of My little ones. You can only add the wealth of My Love by loving with a genuine, simple love, as given to you by Me. Look at your own hearts. Are they white and clean? You strive to enter the narrow gate, but you cannot get through for all of the baggage that you carry.

I ask of you in these Words: come to Me in the nakedness of spirit, with all your feelings, all your fears, everything, My children, and you will find the peace of heart that you seek from Me.

If you live in the earthly ways that you entertain, then all My children will learn from you is earthly ways. But if, within your hearts, you entertain My Ways, then My little ones will have shepherds of Truth and Love, for they shall not see you, but Me, and My Spirit will be alive in you.

Do not frighten My lambs away by your leadership, but attract them by your service and simplicity. There is no greatness in Heaven and you will not gain souls through your anger.

Do not condemn My little ones, as I do not condemn you, and allow them to love Me without fear, for many have been driven away from Me in this way. Do not sit and wait for them to return, but go and seek them. Seek their vulnerability, their love - as they seek yours.

Accept these Words as Words of wisdom from One who is Wisdom itself. Begin to believe again in simple faith and love, and My Spirit will live in you. Do not complicate Him, and many shall be the miracles of healing that I shall perform through you. Are these Words a hard teaching? Will you walk away from Me by carrying on in the way that you now live? Ask yourselves this question: is My Church, My Body, dying because of you? Look in faith at My Truth (not yours) and tell Me your answer.

Or are these Words in vain?

CHAPTER 7

THE REALITY OF LOVE

Ah, children, come with Me and together We will look at the world and I will tell you the Truth of the many questions that you ask of Me.

You say, "I do not believe that God would let all the wars, famines, earthquakes and many other disasters happen." This is true, My little ones, I do not wish it. It is your complacency, your unlove, that allows all these things to happen.

My children, look! Have I not provided enough food for all of My children? But greed overcomes.

These Words, I can see that you do not want to listen to, because they are the Truth. My children, what I would ask is that you look into your own homes. Are you short of food? No, children, all that you find in shortage is the fineries of this world. Children, is it not true that your dreams are of the finer things in life - houses, cars, holidays, and most important to you, money?

Do you ever cast a thought towards My little starving children, or can you not see the Truth? Or will you not see the Truth?

Complacency is a vile thing that the evil one has cast over all of My children. And it is you, in your free will, who have let him in. Have I not already Warned you of this in My Word *(Scripture)*? Do not turn the blame upon your brother or Me, but, My little ones, I ask you, as you read these Words, to look into your own life and find the Truth of these Words that I speak to you. I do not blame or condemn, but I simply ask that you look, so that We, together, may begin to change the things that are not of Me.

Do not be worried, but take this Love that I offer and We will begin again.

Children, you know that I have given all of you free will to be with Me or against Me - there are no in-betweens - you are either for Me, or you are against Me; the choice is yours. I ask, but I cannot force, and all I ask is that you look, and when you decide, I will be waiting for you with open Arms to Love you and cherish you.

Now, children, can you see the truth of the many wars that spring up all over the earth? It is simply greed, a lust for power. Man walks freely into the hands of the evil one. Remember, have I not already told you that he is the father of lies - that he wanders this earth like a roaring lion, ready to snatch any of My children who are ready to listen to his lies?

Look, governments of this world, you have listened to the evil one far too long. Can you not see? It is simple; it is wealth and power that you seek, not Love. You hold My children in bondage in your lust and your greed. Do you think that I will let this continue much longer before I will Touch you with My Justice?

This, I tell you, I do not want to do, but you force My Hand in your own free will.

Do you think that I want this? No, little ones, I simply want to Love you. But, My Justice is My Love and I cannot watch My children suffer at your hands much longer.

Look at the many innocents who suffer torturous deaths in their mothers' wombs. These are My beloved children, of whom millions are murdered each year and only because they will not suit the lifestyles of those who murder them - or because they will be in their way.

My children, do you not realise that the evil one desires human sacrifice in order to gain strength?

See, children, it is freely given to him in ways that you refuse to see. It is, indeed, freely given to him upon this earth by you, My people, in wars, abortions and many other things that are hidden from you, that you would not believe possible were you to be told the Truth.

It is darkness that he feeds upon; the darkness of sin.

Oh, My children, My children, My children, can you not see the truth as it is - that truth which causes the many disasters that you call natural? Do you not see that he desires to cause as much suffering and pain wherever he goes?

Look, children, see the great cities upon the earth. Places where the evil one is allowed to gorge himself on the much darkness of unlove. Look, children, see the places where the great sexual spirits are allowed to roam freely. You can only see these as places of pleasure. See how they blind you and enter you and have free control of you to rape, murder and abuse. They have been allowed to wander this earth freely.

And is it not I who am blamed for allowing these things to happen? Do you see now why I must come in Justice? To cleanse this world of the darkness that you, My people, have invited into My Light.

Now can you see the great Pain that I must endure for Love of you? My Pain is greater when I look around My creation, as the Light of My Love grows dimmer as each day passes. It is I who must carry your pain, for your pain is Mine; your sin is Mine to suffer, and these burn My Heart. It is as though I am placed into a great furnace.

But I will not give up. You do not realise the Love that I have for you. This Heart burns with a profuse Love, an Everlasting Love.

These Words that I have spoken, I know that they do not suit you because they are the Truth. My children, is it not also truth that you refuse to look? Have it known, that I do not speak these Words to condemn, for My Forgiveness is ever-present. All that I do is call to you to seek the Truth, for there you will find the Peace that surpasses all understanding, My Peace, that is contained within My Most Sacred Heart, which I offer freely to you in these Words of Love.

I Love you, I Love you, I Love you. Please hear My calls, I Love you. Come into My Arms, so that you can feel My Loving and tender embrace. I await your answer.

CHAPTER 8

LOVE'S GLORY

Ah, these Words are My Truth. Many of you will look incredulously at them and wonder that I could speak such Words. I, Jesus, tell you that they are all Truth.

It is Love's glory to Touch you with Words of sacredness, for I am the very Word of My Father in Heaven and all I speak are the Words of the One who sent Me, and everything that is His, He has given to Me, and everything that is Mine belongs to Him. I am in the Father and He is in Me. We are One and inseparable. This is Love's Glory.

The Godhead that you perceive in these Words are We in whom you believe - together, merged, One. We are the Holy Spirit. We are the God of Love that is the Creator of All Things. All who believe in Us, We empower with Love to further create Love in the fullness of Our Love. As Love has begotten Love, so Love begets Love. In the realm of Love, We are a constant Love. All things have their being in Us and through Us. We are tenderness and joy and Peace and it is given to all mankind.

Heaven is a place that you could not perceive in your earthliness, and revealed to you this day are the treasures, for its treasures are Us. We are your Salvation. We are your Source. We are your reward for love. All Heaven is Us and We are Heaven.

Our Being is Love. There is no other thing within Us and no sin or darkness can enter the threshold of Our Being. Forgiveness is Our Way of bringing Light into a place of darkness. The Light is born of Love and the Light expels the darkness, for it comes as the Bridegroom in search of His Bride. It opposes all darkness and manifests itself in the soul. The soul is touched by a mêlée of Light, flooding, drowning the soul in Love's perfection, for We are perfection itself.

Believe, man, therefore, for it is the God of Love who would speak with you. IT IS WE, THE TRIUNE GOD, who would speak through these two souls in this way. We who are goodness, Mercy and Almighty, offer Redemption to the world in these Words - and in these, the last days of your era. We, in Our Godhead, ask that these Words be spread among ALL mankind - for they are Our Words, and no man can take anything away from them, nor add anything to them.

The Book of Life is open and We, in Our compassion, are allowing many of Our Words to flow like rivers, waterfalls of Love, into this world. We are breathing life into the nostrils of ALL who would listen, for soon We will come to rid the world of ALL evil, for evil has overcome almost all of what We have seen fit to create.

Mankind has allowed darkness to enter where the Light is, and We will come to take it away. Anyone who does not live in the Light will perish. Anyone who does not believe, is condemned already. Man's complacency has driven many stakes into the Heart of Us and, in Our compassion, We offer the amnesty of Our Forgiveness, for We are total in Our compassion and Our Forgiveness.

We ask that you return to Us within a time and two times and half a time for this time ticks on. We have not created time, but man has, and so We give him this time.

These are not new Words, but Words that have already been spoken by Us and they are the Words of Our Mouth that We speak. These are the Words of a God that Loves with much compassion, but We will, in Our Mercy, Forgive, if mankind is willing to listen to these Words. These, creation, are Words of Apocalypse and these are given to you to love. In Mercy, We have spoken through Our Disciple of Love *(Saint John the Evangelist)*, and these precious Words We have uttered and they have not listened.

We speak these Words to every man and woman, lay and consecrated alike, for all have fallen short, even in Salvation, of Our glory. We Come soon.

CHAPTER 9

WORDS OF TRUTH

Truth, I shall give you, My children. The words of this section have not yet been fulfilled, only mankind can write these words...

ACCOMPANYING MESSAGES

ACCOMPANYING MESSAGES

From the Great Mother of God

My children, I, your Mother, come to Love you and to surround you with this Mantle. It will protect you from harm.

I come also, in these Words, to implore all of you to begin to take My Son seriously. Many times you do not. If you could see Him as I see Him. His Heart is so filled with Love that it tears Him into shreds. The Pain is unbearable at this time more than any other, for the world simply ignores His cries.

But soon, all you shall hear is a deathly stillness, for He shall not call any more for it will be the end of Mercy Time. He has given the world more than it needed.

The Anguish of My Son will come in a great Cry of Pain that will reverberate throughout the world and the sound will be terrible. Listen for the sound of His Voice within you at this time, children, for He needs your love.

From Saint Thérèse of Lisieux

Little children of Jesus, I love you. I have been allowed to come in these Words to greet you. I will tell you the Words that are in my heart to tell you.

Jesus Loves this world, yet they cannot see Him. He is misjudged, by even the people who say that they belong to Him. I say to you that you must simply love Him. Love Him with all the little things and these shall be the stairway that reaches up to Heaven before you, as it was for me.

Jesus is ALL; love Him.

From Saint Margaret Mary Alacoque

My brothers and sisters, the Heart of Jesus is an open Wound; it is Love. His Heart desires souls to quench His great Thirst. Immerse yourselves into Him and you shall never regret it. His Love is sweet when you find it. It is like the sweet nectar and can only be sipped at to know its taste.

Bear all things well for the sake of His Love, as He bore, with great Suffering, the Cross for our sake. Bear it lovingly, for He bore us with His Body, His Blood, His Divinity and with His very Soul.

I urge you to love Him and know the depth of Him. He is an Ineffable Sweetness. Linger with Him and love Him.

Saint Michael the Archangel and the Heavenly Hosts of Angels

Greetings, brothers and sisters. I, Michael, Archangel of the Lord Jesus, come to tell you of the many Words that our Master has spoken.

These are great Words of Love and Pain. Do you not see the Truth of these Words? Or do you refuse to look?

We, the Heavenly Hosts, tell you through our brother, Michael, that great sadness has befallen us as we watch our beautiful Saviour, Jesus, Suffer.

We plead with you, children of God, to look and see what the evil one is doing and the freedom you are giving to him.

Do you not realise, or is it true that you do not want to?

Children of God, if you call upon our assistance, we, the Mighty Hosts will come and do battle in your name and lead you back upon the path of Truth.

Come. I, Michael and My brothers, make this plea. Blessings, children, in the Name of Jesus, who is ALL. Do not forget to praise and love such a powerful God. All love and peace be upon you, children of God.

From Saint Peter, Apostle

Children, do you not see what this world is doing to Jesus? The Pain that He Suffers; it is as if He were being crushed in a great wine press, a million times a second. Yet, He still Loves on.

Remember, children, He is ALL Forgiveness, no matter what you have done or said. His Arms are ALWAYS open. Ask and it shall be given; seek and you shall find; knock and the door shall be opened.

Remember I, Peter, denied Him three times in His time of great need; yet, He Loved and Forgave me.

So come, children, do not be afraid to enter by the narrow gate. You cannot imagine what awaits you. The great Joy, Peace and Love is beyond what any human could comprehend. All you have to do is ask.

I love all of you. Brothers and sisters are we in the Lord Jesus. I love you; call upon me and I will help.

The Four Great Angels of the Apocalypse

Children of God, this day, our Master, Jesus, has given us permission to speak. We are the Avenging Angels. We come to tell you that our time is soon here. Already we have drawn our swords. We will come striking at all evil.

Know, mankind, that you have flown in the Face of God too long.

When the time of Mercy has ended, it shall be our time. No evil shall escape us. It has been allowed to seep into every corner unhindered.

Be Warned, children of God! We are not mythical as many of you tend to think.

These Words we speak to cardinals, bishops, priests and laity alike. If you do not carry the Seal of Jesus, you will not escape us. Those of you, who do have the Seal, we will defend. We tell you, you do not realise what is about to befall mankind. You are either for Jesus or you are against Him.

Do not take these Words lightly. Love is our aim. All evil must go. Farewell, brothers and sisters, please listen. We love you. Hail and praise to Jesus. All Blessings be upon Him. Let His Name be ever on your lips in thanksgiving. Amen.

SELECTED
PRAYERS

SELECTED PRAYERS

CHAPLET OF LOVE

Given by Jesus
17 January 1995

My sons, and all My children, say this Chaplet of Love for Me and let it be given to My Heart with all the love and sincerity that is in you and it, too, will appease My Pain in this time of great tribulation and Sorrow that is in Me. Say it now at the Hour of Justice (6pm) and say it continually through the three days of darkness while I rebuild the world with Love. It will stem the flow of My Tears that are cried eternally for this world. Through it, amass a great vessel of love, so that I may drink it so as to quench My Thirst for souls, for a good number will be saved through it. Say it for your families and for your priests. Say it for yourselves and all of My children and I will hear it and be moved to grant many miracles through it. Say it on My Mother's jewels. Say these Words:

First:
On the Crucifix: Kiss the Cross of Love and say:
O, Most Adorable Heart, I love Thee. Save us.

Second:
On the first large bead (after the Cross):
O, Most Sacred Heart, I love Thee profoundly.
Pour upon us Thy Merciful Love.

Third:
On the next three beads:
Jesus, Heart of Tenderness,
save the hearts that do not love Thee.

Fourth:
On the next large bead:
O Most Sacred Heart, I love Thee profoundly.
Pour upon us Thy Merciful Love.

Fifth:
On the medal:
Infinite Love, fill us so that we may love Thee profoundly.

Sixth:
On each large bead between the decades:

O Great Vessel of Love, that holds only Love, offer to the Father of All, the little love that I give, to appease the Pain that is in Thy Most Sacred Heart, that He may see the profound Love and save us in His infinite Mercy.

Seventh:
On the small decade beads:
O, Jesus, Heart of Love, I love Thee,
let my love appease Thy Pain.

End:
Pray the fifth, fourth, third, second and first stages on the appropriate medal, beads and Cross.

PRAYER OF LOVE

Jesus, I greet You with my heart and my soul, my body, my mind, my understanding, my intellect and my will and I give it all to You. Jesus, I love You a billion times; and may each "I love You" become a little dart, flaming with the Fire of Your Divine Love, and may it pierce the most inner depths of Your Heart - then You will know that it is I, and I love You.

PRAYER OF COMMITMENT

Jesus, my Lord and my God, take my hands and use them as Your own. Use them, Sweet Jesus, to bind up my brothers' wounds, so that in turn I might bind up Yours. Take also my feet, that You might walk in my footsteps to travel this world bringing Your Gospel of Love to all Your children, so that they might see Your Love. My lips, Lord, are Yours, that they might tell - by every word that I speak - of how You Died on the Cross so that all could be Loved. By means of this little prayer, my Jesus, I, from this time forward, belong to You. Amen.

PRAYER OF CONSECRATION AND RENEWAL

O Sacred Heart of Jesus, I place all my trust in Thee. Help me never to falter in this life that You Yourself have chosen for me. Light this path so that I may not stumble. I give You my love, my heart, my soul and my life, so that You might do with them what You will. I give You my sufferings, so that they might help to appease Your Pain. Every part of me is Yours to use for the Salvation of souls. My Jesus, I consecrate my whole being to You and I ask You to accept my humble offering. In Your holy and precious Name, I go out into this world to spread Your Love. Amen.

PRAYER TO OUR LADY, MOTHER OF LOVE DIVINE

Sweet and gentle Mother, hail, my Queen. Open Thy Heart of Love and Grace to Thy children this day. Never let us stray from the Most Sacred Heart of Thy Dear Son, nor Thy most holy and Immaculate Heart. Be our light in this ever-darkening world. Be our light that shines in our hearts, so that Thy Son may never pass us by. We pledge ourselves to Thy most Loving Son and Thee, our dear Mother of Love Divine. Take us to Him, present us to Him; let us kneel at His Feet. Keep us ever serving, ever loving, so that we might appease His Pain. Amen.

CONSECRATION TO THE UNITED HEARTS OF JESUS AND MARY

Here I stand before You in my nothingness. I have nothing, only what You give me, Most Sacred Heart of Jesus and my Mother Immaculate. Here I stand weeping for the sins of the world. I weep for my own. Through these sins, I am united to You, for You have Died on the Cross of Your Love for me. I give You, United Hearts, this heart of mine to be united to Yours. Take this small heart and unite it to Yours, my sweet Jesus, my sweet Mother. In Your Pain, allow me to appease it in some small way. I consecrate all that I am, all that I have, into Your two Hearts, which are filled with sweet and ineffable Love. Let my little love be bound with Your two Hearts. Let this offering be a fragrance that is pleasing to the Father of all Light and Love. Let me be this sacrifice to gain many souls so as to quench Your insatiable thirst for souls. May I always be offered in this sacrifice to these United Hearts, forever. Amen.

MORNING PRAYER

Jesus, to Your Most Sacred Heart I give myself this day, to be a sacrifice of love to You; a victim of Your Love. Pierce my heart with this Arrow of Love, that I may begin and end this day with You. I love You, my Sweet Saviour, my King, and this day is for You. Amen.

PRAYER FOR HELP IN THE DARKNESS

My Jesus, I humbly ask that You surround me, my family, my loved ones and all mankind, with Your Most Precious Blood. I call upon Your most holy Angels through this most simple prayer of love. Thank You, Jesus.

O great Angels, servants of the Most High, come to me in my time of need. I, a simple sinner, call upon you, who are the true servants of our Master, Jesus Christ. I humbly plead that you do battle against the evil one for me, my family, my loved ones, and all mankind. In my gratefulness I will love the Lord, my God, with my whole heart and soul and mind and body and my neighbour as myself, as you do. Amen.

NOVENA PRAYER
TO THE MOST SACRED HEART OF JESUS
Wednesday 26 July 1995

My children, it is good to see you gathered here with Me. I am with you. I am in the Bread and Wine and I am within your souls. I need much love from you, for My Heart is torn by many things. Love this Heart, children, whose constant cry is Love, whose Tears are Love. I create and I destroy; I design, I build and I am building you into My Love. I cry for your hearts, for they are Mine.

These Words of prayer I give you within the walls of this house[1], for I wish to honour it, as it honours Me. I am constant in My affection for all who dwell within it and it is on their account that I give this Love.

Say this prayer for Me, for it is wrought from the Pain. Say it to obtain the impossible and I will rend My own Flesh to give you what you ask for. Say it over a period of eight days, honouring this Heart with your love as you say it.

It is a prayer of tender love for My sake and My sake alone.

[1] This is not the House of Prayer in Cookstown.

** This Novena Prayer is given by Jesus to be said at any time. There is no set time to say it. After every prayer He asks that we make an Act of Faith by saying the Apostles Creed.
He asks that we go to confession any time within this eight days and receive Him in the Blessed Sacrament on the last day as an act of love and faith before we say the last part.
In this Prayer Jesus asks that the Words be said with much love in our hearts for Him and that we say it meaningfully.

First day   My Good Jesus, I immerse myself into Your Most Grieved and Painful Heart. I penetrate it with my little love. I desire to give my heart this day to be consumed in Love by You. *Say the Apostle's Creed*

Second day   O my Loving Jesus, immerse me into this Heart of Goodness so that I may comfort You from the coldness of men. Give me the Grace to love You above all things. O Burning Abyss, I have so little a love to give, but it is a tender love. Let it trace upon Your Heart a little joy. *Say the Apostle's Creed*

Third day   O Passionate Saviour, I look upon Your Cross of Ineffable Love, of great Suffering and Pain. I see the great Wounds that saved me and gave me life. I can only whisper the words 'I love You.' *Say the Apostle's Creed*

Fourth day   O Sweet Heart that Loves me, how can I accept the sweetness of Your Touch in my life? How can I begin to understand the fathoms of inexhaustible Love? My God and my all! My Good Jesus, I stand before Your Heart, all burning with fiery Love and I am nothing in its Light. I love You, I love You, my God and my all, I love You. *Say the Apostle's Creed*

Fifth day   O Great Heart, I bind my heart to Yours this day and forever. Let me be the victim of its Love, to appease and sacrifice, to repair and to atone for the blasphemies and sacrileges done against it. Let my own life be the atonement to soothe its great Pain. Demand then, from this little heart, the necessary love that will bind it and shield it from the little love of men. *Say the Apostle's Creed*

Sixth day   Torrent of Love, I praise You. Heart of Passion, shed the Light of the fire of Your Being upon me so that I may truly repent of my sinfulness in gratefulness of Your Love of me. I pledge You my love, I pledge You my soul. My God, my God, I love You. *Say the Apostle's Creed*

Seventh day   My God, I hope in You. My God, I believe in You. Let Your great Burning Heart consume me so that I may never again be separated from You. I beg You to hear the request of this humbled heart. Let it join with Yours forever. I do not deserve to be in Your company, but You Yourself have called me through these Words of Love. Abyss of Love consume me, burn me. Sweet Saviour, I adore You, I love You. *Say the Apostle's Creed*

Eighth day   Receive Me respectfully. My Body, My Blood, My Soul and My Divinity.
O Sweet Flesh, All Consuming Love, River that pours into me through this Life-giving Bread, annihilate me and let me ever cling to You. Sacrament of Love, through this which I have received, let it be the return of love that You seek from men. My Lord and my God, I love You, I love You, I love You. *Say the Apostle's Creed*

These Words are for all of you that would love Me, who would atone to Me, who would return love for Love. I Love you, My children. Let all of you here be the bearers of My Words and the gatherers of My Love to return it to Me to appease My Pain. I Love you.

THE TWO PATRICKS
AND
THE HOUSES OF PRAYER

THE TWO PATRICKS

PATRICK RUSHE

In 1985, I began to experience what are termed 'mystical experiences.' I do not know how to describe these in words, as there are no created words that could describe something so beautiful that comes from God. I could try, by using such adjectives as beautiful, wonderful, but these words are insufficient, as a drop of water is in a vast ocean.

Just why Jesus should choose me to bestow these upon, I don't know either. I am just an ordinary person who does ordinary things. I believe in Jesus Christ as a personal God, but I am more than content with what He has given to me in the Catholic Church, and I find great spiritual comfort in it.

These experiences that I speak of, have been described as Saint John of the Cross experiences. Saint John of the Cross was a Spanish mystic, who was a contemporary of the great Saint Teresa of Avila, who founded the discalced Carmelite Order. Saint Teresa is one of the great Doctors of the Church. God gave Saint John many deep and mystical truths. He came to know God through the great darknesses in his life, which brought his soul fully into the Light of God, the Bridehood, union of the soul. He has written many books on the subject, such as Dark Night of the Soul, and many poems of his longings for his Beloved. The one that I feel best describes my own experiences is The Living Flame of Love.

These experiences, which I am still having, are to do with the deep, inner things of the soul – things I know nothing about; but it seems that I am experiencing them. I did not go seeking these, but it appears that they have been placed within me – infused into me – for I have had no knowledge of these hidden things, until I began asking what was happening to me.

From about 1985 – 1991, I told no one about them because I could not put into words what went on deep within me. Then I told a local priest as these Touches of Jesus, or ecstasies, were becoming so strong and intense, that I thought many times that I was going to die in them. If you can imagine someone turning on a shower directly above your head and the water pouring, not only over your body, but completely filling your mind, will, intellect and soul. I felt as though I was on fire, being totally consumed, burned, eaten up and deeply, deeply Loved.

The first time that this happened, it lasted approximately fifteen minutes. Since then, they can last anything from one hour to – as happened once – two weeks.

It would take too long to describe these touches – as I call them – but each one is different. They come in different intensities. Some are so gentle that I can hardly know that they are there, while others are strong, yet bearable; and again, others are so intense that I feel that my heart will explode, or that only death will relieve it. Jesus, in these Touches, invades me with something that I cannot relate to anyone. All I know is that He does not know when to stop.

These can also come in great longings for Jesus, when my soul thirsts for Him. Nothing upon this earth can satisfy these longings – nothing. These fill me, and are somehow different from the 'Touches'. They are compelling, like a pain or a thirst. All of these can come at any time. There is no warning, and I do not have to be at prayer. In the beginning, these longings came just before receiving the Eucharist, and I felt nothing could have stopped me from receiving Jesus.

After I had shared with my local curate, he advised me to seek spiritual guidance from someone with experience in these matters. As I was looking for this, I spoke to a Sister in the parish. She confirmed what I had been told, and I was bewildered by all of this.

The communications with Jesus were not yet in Message form, only Touches, and I had no way of knowing what He wanted of me, if indeed anything.

My prayer life, at this stage, had developed and deepened and great urges at times overwhelmed me and called me to prayer. It was as though I was entirely wrapped in Jesus, and I felt a deep, intimate relationship with Him.

Prayer took on newness at this time. It seemed that, if I made any move to pray, Jesus took over. He called me into His world. Although I was still basically aware of what was going on around me, I was lost to this world. He was consuming me, instilling me with Love. I began my prayer with a simple 'I love You, Jesus,' and I was enveloped by Him.

I asked the Sister's advice because I could not pray vocally and, up to this point, I believed that vocal prayer *was prayer*. She advised me to read Scripture, as it was a form of prayer. Then she said to read a passage and absorb it and, for about fifteen minutes, to do something else. After this, I was to return and write down any thoughts that I may have had.

I took this advice and tried it. For the first two days, it seemed to go the way Sister had said. On the third day the thoughts that I was writing down were coming like prophecy. I could not understand this and I became afraid and stopped immediately. I did not feel comfortable.

About a week or so later, I spoke with the nun again and told her my fears. I showed her the writings, and she told me not to be afraid, and to carry on. I then remembered that, during a Touch about a year before this, I had had a great urge to write. It was compelling me to write, even though I tried to ignore it and push it away. I finally had to do it. When it was written, I did not look at it. I went and hid it. I did not know what to do. This was the beginning of the Messages, and many people might think that they would be delighted to be in this position. It did not affect me in this way. I was uncomfortable with it. When I began to realise that they were communications from Jesus, I could not believe it, and I began to ask Him to remove it, because I was afraid. I had great doubts. I do not, for one moment, doubt the Power of God, but I doubted my own capability.

From there, I moved on through two Spiritual Directors, hoping that one of them would tell me it was wrong. They gave me tremendous help.

The Messages continued and about one and a half to two years later, the Spiritual Director of this time gave me leave to speak openly about the Messages, and share them. Except through friends, I did not know how to begin to do what Jesus was asking in the Messages. One night, I went to Kilnacrott Abbey, Co. Cavan, to do an all-night vigil there. I met with a man who was promoting devotional medals. I did not realise that he was also called very deeply by Jesus, and that the Lord had great Plans for him also. We did not speak at length, and it was a month later when he telephoned me to find out more about the Messages of Love. The man's name was Patrick O Kane.

We spoke for about two hours on the telephone, and arranged to meet a few days later. We met and talked for a long time about the Messages and Patrick told me that he would offer his car to drive me to any meeting, anywhere. I could not believe his great generosity and should have known that the Lord Jesus had His Hand in everything. We soon became great friends and together we went to many prayer meetings at which I'd been invited to speak, not realising that Jesus had also called Patrick to be an equal part of the Messages.

Jesus told me one night in a Message that He wanted Patrick to begin to speak at prayer meetings. His reaction to this was fear. But he obeyed what Jesus had said and began to speak, not only at meetings, but Jesus also gave him the Gift of Prophesy. This was met with bewilderment.

The Ways of Jesus Christ are not our ways. He has told us in many teachings that He, Himself, has brought us together in this mission at different times in our development towards Him, so that we could learn from each other, as well as from Him.

He has described us as two halves of a jewel. It is only when we are one that His Light can shine through us – for anything we do is done in Jesus, for Jesus, and through Jesus.

The Messages of Love are An Invitation to Love Jesus – the Love of His Most Sacred Heart, as given by Him through His Dove, Saint Margaret Mary Alacoque, contained, once more, for our time, in these pages. It is a Love that endures much Pain through Loving us.

The writings of Jesus are full of great tenderness and Love. He is calling us to His Side. He challenges us to be the people that we say we are. He speaks often of His beloved Church and He calls us back

to the Sacraments where His Love is made manifest to us.
Do not just read these Messages, live them.

Patrick Rushe

I always knew God. I knew that He was close to me, but I kept Him at a distance because I thought He was boring. I also knew that I could hear Him – well, not exactly hear Him, but I knew what He was saying within my heart. I ignored Him for most of my life. I knew that He was calling me but I did not want to know.

In 1986, I began to answer the calls, but only because times were hard and I needed Him. He came to my assistance in an unusual way. I had a car accident. At this time He showed me many things. I was in intensive care and very seriously ill. The doctors gave me twenty-four hours to live, but I pulled through, much to their amazement. While still in intensive care and very ill, I felt a great pain flow through my body.

My mother was at my bedside. She told me later that she thought that I was dying at that moment, but a great peace surrounded both of us.

I remember telling her to pray. Then I saw what looked like a veil opening in front of my eyes. Suddenly, I was looking from a great height. I could see my mother and myself below. I could see myself in pain and I could also feel the pain that was in my body. A voice – which came from behind me – said, "Prayer and pain releases souls." I saw what seemed like a cloud in a valley between two mountains. The mountains were like red clay. At the end of the valley there was a wall and behind it was a town with dome-shaped houses and these too were of red clay. The town looked bleak and dismal.

Pieces of the cloud began to break off and float upwards. I could see it was the prayer and the pain that was responsible for this. I felt a feeling of great joy at the sight of it.

I followed the pieces of cloud upwards and they went towards a set of golden gates. I could see inside these a little way. I saw great golden fans that blocked my view and I know that I was not allowed to see further. I realised that the clouds that I had seen were souls being released from Purgatory.

The person, who was behind me said, "All will be revealed to you when you reach this point." Jesus told me later that this 'person' or 'voice' was my Guardian Angel. The 'point' that Nathaniel (my Angel's name) was speaking about was the point of entry into the Kingdom of God.

I was shown many things at this time, but these would be too numerous to mention here. I was told to tell all people to say the Rosary for peace and unity in the world and for the happy repose of souls. I was also told that I would recover soon.

The following day I was taken out of intensive care. Eight days later I was out of hospital, much to the amazement of the doctors and everyone else.

All things began to get better in my life and I went back to work. The money was good, all the bills went and so did God. I had no time for Him, once again. I suppose that this is the way of the world; when we are in trouble we want Gods help. He does help and all things go well; then He begins to get in the way. This is the way it happened with me. I would take 'holy fits,' now and again; I would say my prayers and go to Mass. Most times I did not even want to go to Mass, I was too busy living. Going to Mass and saying prayers did not really fit because it made me feel guilty. I knew that I was not doing right by Jesus. I knew that He was still calling.

I liked to hear about various Messages from around the world especially if they were about the chastisements. The harsher the better, but still I did not change my life. I went on.

One day I was passing the chapel in my hometown and I went in. To this day I do not know why. I went in, walked up to the altar of Our Lady and sat down. I knew that Jesus was there. I said to Him, "I haven't said the Rosary in years, but I'll have a go anyway." I knew that there was one Our Father, ten Hail Marys and one Glory be to the Father. I could not remember the Mysteries so I said to Jesus, "You do the Mysteries and I will say the prayers", and this is what We did.

As I was coming out of the chapel I found a leaflet about the Divine Mercy and took it with me. I asked my wife, Pauline, to read it to me as I have dyslexia and do not read or write well. I was very interested in the contents of the leaflet. I went to the chapel again the next day and said the Chaplet of Divine Mercy from the leaflet. Then I discovered a leaflet about the Rosary on the seat next to me. Jesus was leaving nothing to chance. He began to teach me about Himself and His Mother. He placed a great hunger in me for Himself that could not be satisfied. There is a saying about people "eating the altar rails." I would have eaten the rails, the altar and all.

I loved Jesus and Mary so much that all I wanted to do was spend time in the chapel at every service that was going. I went there every evening after work. This went on for about five months. Then the longing left, all was gone. I knew that Jesus was telling me that He had helped me but now I was to see what I could do by myself.

The search for Him began. I got Messages from all over the world. I listened to every religious tape I could find over and over again. I went to Mount Mellory in Ireland more than twenty times. Everyone was seeing different things there but I saw nothing spiritual but I always felt great Peace there. My consolation was a great love for the Rosary. I said it at every opportunity, before work, at lunchtime and in the evenings. It was a refuge that Our Lady had given to me. Thank You, Mary, for this beautiful Gift.

I found a great love for the Messages that Jesus and Mary gave through an Irish Visionary. Through this association I met two beautiful people. They helped me so much that I could see the love they had for God. They gave me many leaflets and prayers to distribute and promote. This was the beginning of my wanting to work for God. One of these ladies gave me thousands of leaflets, medals and tapes to distribute. I found a small satisfaction in my hunger by doing this. I thank Jesus for these two ladies. May Jesus Bless them and their families for the good that they did for me and many others.

I did this work for a long time but I could not find what I had in those previous five months. One night I went to Kilnacrott Abbey in Co. Cavan to do an all night vigil there. A friend called Kevin Quinn introduced me to Patrick Rushe. Patrick was receiving Messages. I said to him that I would like to talk to him but something strange happened. He walked one way and I walked the other. Neither of us knew why this happened but we have guessed that Jesus had something to do with it.

About a month later, I rang Kevin to get Patrick's telephone number. When I rang him we spoke for about two and a half hours. We arranged to meet a few days later. Patrick had no transport and had no way of spreading the Messages. I offered my help and we began going to prayer meetings where Patrick would speak. I was quite happy to drive and spread the Messages. I had no way of knowing but it had begun.

Jesus had begun to speak to me through Patrick and He asked me to speak Words of Prophecy. I did not want to do this but Jesus kept asking. I was afraid but finally I said yes. I was afraid of my own humanness and that I would mislead His people. Jesus spoke with great gentleness and patience to His children, and always the Words were about His great Love. I felt alright about this. One night, Jesus asked me to speak at a meeting. I nearly had a heart attack. I would not know what to say. But Jesus assured me that it would be Him who would do the speaking. They would be His Words and not mine. I spoke for the first time and to my surprise the Words just flowed from me. Although my mind was blank, Words were coming from me; I was saying things that I know that I did not learn. I began to trust Jesus and I began to feel comfortable with what I was doing. But I still had to learn that Jesus never gives up.

Jesus asked me to write His Words. I did not want this. Enough was enough. As I said earlier I have dyslexia and I find difficulty in reading and writing. Jesus explained in a Message to both of us. He said He had placed a jewel in this world and His Work could not be done unless the two halves of the jewel were together, and His Light shining through it. All we would have to do is say yes in our free will. He taught us that we, of ourselves, could not do anything for we are sinners, no different to anyone, in spite of the fact that Jesus was speaking to us. Jesus would do the talking. Thank You, Jesus, my

Friend for all that You have done for us. I love You.

Jesus told me that He would help with my fears and my reading and, most of all, my writing; and He did. I still have not found what I had in the earlier five months, and Jesus told me that I would have to go through this 'darkness' so that He could mould me into what He wants me to be. It is difficult at times, but with the help of Jesus and Patrick I keep going, for it is His Will and not mine.

Jesus Christ is ALL, and we are nothing but two sinners, whom Jesus wishes to use. Our lives are nothing, but to Jesus the lives of His children are everything.

I love You, Jesus, and I ask that You give me the Grace to serve You, Your Mother and Your Church in truth, love, humility and obedience. Thank You, Jesus and Mary, for the Love You bestow upon us all. I love You.

Patrick O Kane.

THE SACRED HEART HOUSE OF PRAYER

At prayer on Christmas Eve 1993, Jesus spoke to me interiorly and I heard the words "Procure Me a House..." I heard these words clearly, but they frightened me, so I asked Jesus to speak to me through Scripture. I opened the Jerusalem Bible at random, and the first Words that my eyes fell upon were "...My House shall be called a House of Prayer..."

Again I was afraid, because I realised the implications of what the parish priest might say, and what the bishop might say, so once again I put Jesus to the test.

I opened the Scriptures again and my eyes fell upon the same Words "...My House shall be called a House of Prayer..."

It was very clear what Jesus was trying to tell me – but as if this was not enough, I asked Him again for more proof. By this stage, I was almost beside myself with worry as to what everyone would think. Jesus gave me the same Words from Scripture as He had given before.

I sat there not knowing what to do next, so I telephoned Patrick O'Kane. I told Patrick of what Jesus had said and Patrick said, "...If Jesus wants a House, Jesus will get a House."

We began soon after this to look for a House. We asked various people to look out for any empty houses around Cookstown and to let us know of them.

We looked at different places, but they seemed cold, and we knew that these were not what Jesus wanted. It was very disappointing because we wanted to give Jesus the best that our efforts could give.

On Monday 1 February 1994, Patrick O'Kane received a small parcel and in it was £1,000 in notes. We could not believe it. There was no letter with it, as the person wished to remain anonymous. (We would like, at this time, to thank the person, or persons who sent this money to us. Without it, the Sacred Heart House of Prayer would not have been possible. We pray for you every day. Thank you for listening to Jesus.)

The next day, a good friend (who was assisting in our search for the premises) drew our attention to a house right in the centre of Cookstown. Apparently this house had been empty for about eighteen months.

It was a three-storey house, and we went to see the estate agent, who gave us the keys. As soon as the door opened, both Patrick and I heard the Words from Jesus, "...This is My House..." Then He said, "...My sons, you will not stay here..." By this, Jesus meant that Patrick O'Kane and myself would not spend much time within the House of

Prayer. He had already made it clear that our Mission was to travel around the world to spread the Messages of Love. And He was now telling us that this House would only be our base.

We signed the lease the next day and began the work that needed to be done. There wasn't much for Jesus had said in a Message about a year before this, "...I have gone before you, to prepare..." The House was in very good condition.

About three weeks later, the House was ready for opening. There were many good people – inspired by Jesus – who brought furniture, carpets, statues and pictures. We were ready to open.

In the meantime, Jesus was preparing us for the House opening and He gave various Messages on the subject. He told us that the House was to be a House of Love, a House of Joy, a House of Peace. People were to be welcomed there with love. If they wanted prayer, then there was to be a team of people who would do this. If they preferred to just have a chat, then this was also possible. Jesus told us that no one is to be rejected and that the House is open to all.

Since that time, many gifted people have joined the House to help spread the Gospel of Love. There are about thirty people who make up various teams of prayer, counselling, cleaners, office workers and simply loving people. They are filled with the Holy Spirit and this is seen in the way that they dedicate themselves to the Most Sacred Heart of Jesus and His Plans for His House.

Jesus often refers to the House as His Heart, and many people have been helped to regain their faith, and many have been healed.

It is in the hope of Jesus that His Heart will be the refuge of sinners, the hope of His people in the times of darkness ahead. He calls us to the Way of Love through His Most Beautiful Sacred Heart.

LADY OF THE SACRED HEART HOUSE OF PRAYER

At the end of 1994, we were on tour in England, and we were invited to a house in Wembley, London. There, we met Colleen De Cruz. Jesus told us, as we entered, that this would be another House of Prayer, and that it would be dedicated to His Mother, Mary.

Jesus gave a Message on our second tour of London, and He asked that it be called Lady of the Sacred Heart House of Prayer. It was to be dedicated to Our Lady and its prayer was to be offered for all the victims of abortion. It, too, can be visited at anytime and no one is to be rejected.

One of the things that the Lord has asked for is that, from the Lady of the Sacred Heart House, a team of dedicated people go out into the streets of London, armed with love, sandwiches, tea, coffee, clothes and blankets, and - without criticism or judgement - go feed the hungry, clothe the naked, and give the thirsty a drink. There are many lovely people who are homeless, and Jesus calls us all to do our part.

THE HABIT

It was in November 1995 that Jesus began to speak about a Habit. We did not wish to know anything about it because it seemed to be the most difficult thing that Jesus had ever asked us to do. We began to protest to Him that this was against the Law of the Church, to which He replied the Laws of His Church were written in His Heart and if there was a Law that said we could not wear a Habit then He would have told us. He told us to have the Habit made up and anyone who wished to make a Commitment to it could do so.

At this time the Committee (as it was then called, now the Council) were going to see the bishop and we asked them to ask him if it was against the Law of the Church for us to wear the Habit. His answer to them reflected perfectly the Words that Jesus had spoken, '...there is no Law within the Church to say that you cannot wear a Habit but I advise you to wait a while...' We waited one year. Jesus asked for the inauguration of the Habit to take place on 11 February 1996. And we went ahead with this. Jesus gave us the prayers to say and twenty-five people were committed that day. We did not actually wear the Habit for one full year on the advice of the bishop.

SAINT MICHAEL AND THE HEAVENLY HOSTS HOUSE OF PRAYER

In January 1995 we were asked to talk at a meeting in Tottenham, London. There we met Margaret Gallagher and her son, Thomas. Jesus spoke to Margaret in spoken prophecy about personal things. Next day, Jesus spoke again in prophecy and told us that the House was holy ground and we were standing on holy ground and that this House was His, given to Him by His Mother. Afterwards, Margaret told us that Jesus was really speaking through us because her and her husband had prayed to Our Lady for the House in 1980 and it was Her House.

It was one year before He spoke and then only to ask Margaret did she wish to give it. This Message came out of the blue because sometimes Jesus never answers a question we have asked Him. In it He told Margaret that she was not to give an answer but she was to go to prayer and to think about it. When we telephoned her to read the Message she said, 'yes, yes.' Jesus had given specific Instructions and He wished her to obey them. It was three months before He spoke again to say that He had accepted her house as a House of Prayer. He spoke in a Message that it was to be named Saint Michael and the Heavenly Hosts House of Prayer, and the prayers there were to be offered for priests.

There are now five members of the Habit in the House of Prayer in Tottenham who also have a role in their area to feed the homeless and much good work is carried out by them.

SAINT MARGARET MARY HOUSE OF PRAYER

In January 1996, we were invited to Spain for the first time by a lady called Brenda Allen. Apart from one private meeting in Gibraltar, the meetings were for English/Irish residents. Jesus made it known through the Messages that He wanted to build a bridge of Love between the foreign residents and the Spanish people and He wished to do it through An Invitation To Love Jesus. In July 1996, Brenda was introduced to Romano Petri and his wife, Clara. Romano, a retired translator, was the answer to the biggest problem - the language barrier.

In September 1997, Brenda received a Message from Jesus, requesting a House of Prayer dedicated to Saint Margaret Mary Alacoque. In October 1997, Un Invitacion A Amar A Jesus was registered in Malaga and Madrid as a charity and registered group. In December 1998, permission was found for the Casa De Oracion De Santa Margarita Maria which opened officially on 6 February 1999 with much help and financial support from two other people[1].

We now have a monthly bulletin published in Spanish. Also available in Spanish, An Abyss of Love and Pain and Book One and Two of the Messages of Love.

[1] At the time of publication, this House is closed due to circumstances beyond our control. However, there is a search for another House in this area in Spain being made and until it is found, the way of the Sacred Heart lives on in the hearts of those servants who worked at that House.

SOLITUDE

In 1996, Jesus requested a House of Prayer for Garabandal as Garabandal is the second calling to the servants of the Way of the Sacred Heart. In 2001 this House was purchased in Cosio, about three miles from Garabandal. It is called 'Solitude' because as Jesus said, silence is dear to His Heart. The work there is ongoing and we hope soon to have it completed.

Jesus has already proved that Solitude is a teaching ground where He will teach many. The main teaching to come from Solitude is: we must come to realise that this is a spiritual battle we fight, not a human one. Until we fully realise this then we CANNOT deepen our relationship with Jesus.

BETHLEHEM HOUSE OF PRAYER

Bethlehem House of Prayer is a House of Prayer that Jesus asked for so that it would be a place of retreat and rest for all servants. A certain part of the year is to be used for this. Servants going there would take part in the work and prayer. It is situated in County Donegal.

SHRINE OF THE SACRED HEART OF MARY HOUSE OF PRAYER

This House of Prayer is in Ireland. It is being established as this Book is being printed. The only information we can give you presently, is the Message that Jesus gave.

Patrick:
Jesus, I think I hear You calling me.
Jesus:
Yes, My servant, I have called you to tell you of My House in the town of Drogheda. This House, like My Sacred Heart, will be devoted to My Heart. I request that this House be as My Heart in all things. I ask that its establishment be devoted to My Mother's Sacred Heart and it shall be known as Shrine of the Sacred Heart of Mary. As My Mother only promotes Me in all things then those there will promote devotion to My Most Sacred Heart, that not only the laity but priests and bishops and nuns will return to the devotion. My daughter, Margaret Mary, will be its Patroness and its meditations should be, after My Messages of Love, on the Word that I gave to her.
I do this because it is the time and I wish to establish devotion in this ancient town of faith. It is all but lost in the forest of new age teachings. When the House is found I will speak further. Thank you, My servant, for listening to these Words. Tell few about this until it is established for they will try to stop it. I ask you to do this in obedience because there are many within My Heart who gossip and gossip is a spirit who destroys lives and many of My Plans. Do this for Me. I Love you. *Tuesday 22 April 2003*

HOUSE OF THE ANGELS

While the Patricks were working at a House of Prayer in Ireland, they were offered a property that would possibly be suitable as another House of Prayer and Jesus said yes. Our Lady gave this Message about the House *"...Accept the House that has been offered as a place of the Angels. It should be a place of prayer and vigils, a place to process and should be called, 'House of Angels.' Habits will not be worn there but people should be invited to pray there..." (Saturday 19 June 2004)*
At the time of publication, this House is being established.

HOUSE OF PRAYER IN FRANCE

An inspiration was given to the two Patricks while they were driving through France that there was to be a House of Prayer there, however Jesus did not speak of this House until Wednesday 6 October 2004, when He said, *"...I instruct My two sons in these Words to go and find My House in My country of France for it is further behind than it should be. The purge of communism has ravished this daughter of Mine long enough. I call on those who can help financially in this to do so for I wish to establish My Sacred Heart in this daughter of Mine. Let your hearts be opened to these Words for it is time to start running instead of walking. I ask all of you who read these Words to treat them as urgent for there is danger ahead for those people living in this country. They lose their grip on Me. Are you with Me on this, My children? Then stand up and be counted.*

I speak these Words on this day because they are urgent. This House must be founded within a distance from the capital.

Come and help Me, My children, I would not ask if France were not in danger. I Love you and I appeal to you."

At the time of publication, this House is being searched for.

HOUSES OF PRAYER YET TO BE ESTABLISHED

East London
Manchester
Madrid
America

The Plan of Jesus, in these Messages, is Love. That we take His Love and give it to all peoples, creeds, colours and witness to His Way of Truth, Love and Peace. This is the aim of the Houses of Prayer, and we need many people to come and help us.

We thank Jesus that He gives all of us the Graces to carry His great Plans through. We need the prayers and support of many to help us to fulfil what Jesus has asked of us.

SELECTED
RECENT
MESSAGES

Do you love My priests?
Wednesday 19 April 1995

Look, My children, look at My priests, what do you see? Do you see My servants or do you see men to be despised and rejected? Do you love My priests or do you judge and criticise them? Do you not realise that these too, are My children who need to be loved? They cry out for love, but all they receive is much rejection and loneliness.

O, My children, My children, can you not see? Can you not see that they are forced to seek love in the ways of this world? You say that My priests do not understand; this, My children, is because of the many walls of rejection that they have felt and these they have learned to hide behind. The pain in their hearts is great. They are left defenseless and easy prey for the evil one.

Rise up, My little ones, love My servants. Pray much for them, for in doing this they will begin to see once again. Then you, My children, you, will begin to see the warmth and love that I have placed within them for you, My people. Do not allow the evil one to snatch them from Me by your complacency, unlove and self-righteousness; but love them and begin to understand the mammoth task that they face in bringing My Love to all of you. Love them; please do not reject them. I Love all of you, My children, I Love you. Please do as I ask.

Remember that My bishops, cardinals and My Pope are My priests. Love them as I am Loving you.

Look at the Laws of My Church
Sunday 20 August 1995

Children of this world, I, Jesus, wish to speak to you of My servant, John Paul. Little ones, I ask you to look at the Laws that he has laid down. ARE THEY NOT MY LAWS? If they are not, then where are the Words that I spoke to My Peter, 'What you bind upon this earth it is bound in Heaven; what you loose upon this earth is loosed in Heaven' or, children, will you deny that I spoke these Words?

You do not want to listen to the words of truth, the words of life that My servant speaks, for they are My Words. Blind and foolish generation, you do not want to listen, because the Laws of My Body do not suit your selfish lifestyle. I tell you, deny My servant and you deny Me, your God.

Yes, children, I, Yahweh, Sabaoth, Warn you, you who speak out against My servant, and I speak to you who call yourselves My cardinals, My bishops, My priests, My religious, My laity - you offend your God; blaspheme in My Face. Do you think I will listen to you much longer? Read My Word, Revelation 15 and 16 and be Warned.

1 Then I saw another sign in heaven, great and marvellous: seven angels having the seven last plagues, for in them the wrath of God is complete.

2 And I saw something like a sea of glass mingled with fire, and those who have the victory over the beast, over his image and over his mark and over the number of his name, standing on the sea of glass, having harps of God.

3 They sing the song of Moses, the servant of God, and the song of the Lamb, saying:

"Great and marvelous are Your works, Lord God Almighty! Just and true are Your ways, O King of the saints!

4 Who shall not fear You, O Lord, and glorify Your name? For You alone are holy. For all nations shall come and worship before You, for Your judgments have been manifested."

5 After these things I looked, and behold, the temple of the tabernacle of the testimony in heaven was opened.

6 And out of the temple came the seven angels having the seven plagues, clothed in pure bright linen, and having their chests girded with golden bands.

7 Then one of the four living creatures gave to the seven angels seven golden bowls full of the wrath of God who lives forever and ever.

8 The temple was filled with smoke from the glory of God and from His power, and no one was able to enter the temple till the seven plagues of the seven angels were completed.

Revelation 15

1 Then I heard a loud voice from the temple saying to the seven angels, "Go and pour out the bowls of the wrath of God on the earth."

2 So the first went and poured out his bowl upon the earth, and a foul and loath-some sore came upon the men who had the mark of the beast and those who worshiped his image.

3 Then the second angel poured out his bowl on the sea, and it became blood as of a dead man; and every living creature in the sea died.

4 Then the third angel poured out his bowl on the rivers and springs of water, and they became blood.

5 And I heard the angel of the waters saying:

"You are righteous, O Lord, the One who is and who was and who is to be, because You have judged these things.

6 For they have shed the blood of saints and prophets, and You have given them blood to drink. For it is their just due."

7 And I heard another from the altar saying, "Even so, Lord God Almighty, true and righteous are Your judgments."

8 Then the fourth angel poured out his bowl on the sun, and power was given to him to scorch men with fire.

9 And men were scorched with great heat, and they blasphemed the name of God who has power over these plagues; and they did not repent and give Him glory.

10 Then the fifth angel poured out his bowl on the throne of the beast, and his kingdom became full of darkness; and they gnawed their tongues because of the pain.

11 They blasphemed the God of heaven because of their pains and their sores, and did not repent of their deeds.

12 Then the sixth angel poured out his bowl on the great river Euphrates, and its water was dried up, so that the way of the kings from the east might be prepared.

13 And I saw three unclean spirits like frogs coming out of the mouth of the dragon, out of the mouth of the beast, and out of the mouth of the false prophet.

14 For they are spirits of demons, performing signs, which go out to the kings of the earth and of the whole world, to gather them to the battle of that great day of God Almighty.

15 "Behold, I am coming as a thief. Blessed is he who watches, and keeps his garments, lest he walk naked and they see his shame."

16 And they gathered them together to the place called in Hebrew, Armageddon.

17 Then the seventh angel poured out his bowl into the air, and a loud voice came out of the temple of heaven, from the throne, saying, "It is done!"

18 And there were noises and thunderings and lightnings; and there was a great earthquake, such a mighty and great earthquake as had not occurred since men were on the earth.

19 Now the great city was divided into three parts, and the cities of the nations fell. And great Babylon was remembered before God, to give her the cup of the wine of the fierceness of His wrath.

20 Then every island fled away, and the mountains were not found.

21 And great hail from heaven fell upon men, each hailstone about the weight of a talent. Men blasphemed God because of the plague of the hail, since that plague was exceedingly great.

Revelation 16

My children, I speak to you of My Eucharist. You fight and squabble with one another over whether it is right to receive Me on your hand or on your tongue. I tell you, look at the Laws of My Church and this is your answer, for you cause Me much Pain. It is I whom you fight over in your self-righteousness.

Look and see the Truth; the evil one uses you to split My Church over the very thing you say you love - My Body, My Blood, My Soul and My Divinity. Have you become so blind that you will allow him to do this? Look again, children, are you like the Scribes and the Pharisees - white on the outside and black on the inside? I tell you, simply obey My Laws and you do My Will. I Love you, My children, please believe this.

Pray, pray, pray, for My servant, for they who are not of Me begin to close the snare on My servant, your Holy Father. Believe that My Pope is in much danger from those servants of the evil one; those freemasons who disguise themselves in the robes of My Body.

Please, please help My servant. Thank you, My children, that you have listened. I, your Jesus, Love you.

These next Messages have been kept secret, as requested by Jesus. They are now being released at His request. No explanation has been given by Him as to what He means. Until Jesus gives this explanation, we do not feel that we can comment on it.

My servant, John Paul, will be put off his throne
Sunday 13 November 1994

My sons, I call you together so that I could tell you of things to come, so that you may know that I have spoken of them before they happen. I speak in plain Words, so that you will understand.

Soon you will hear of wars that will break out in countries near and far. To name but a few N-- ----, P----, L-----, will be badly hit, for these things have been in the evil one's plans for a long time.

My people will cry out for Me but I will not be able to help them, for they have chosen to live in the way of the evil one.

My servant, John Paul, will be put off his Throne and there you will see the abomination sitting upon it. You will recognise him by the way that he walks. All this, My sons, will happen within three times three. Do not be alarmed, for the days are numbered.

Already the nuclear weapons are primed in secret. This is known only to the henchmen of the evil one. These henchmen have been strategically placed within all the countries of this world. They even pierce My own Body.

Cardinals, at this time, plot the overthrow of My Pope. Many parts of My Body are about to be changed. They have already begun to weaken him.

Watch, My sons; read what My servant Matthew *(Chapter 24)* has written of My Words; link this with the first six chapters of My Revelation to the world. Do this, My sons, now.

1 Then Jesus went out and departed from the temple, and His disciples came up to show Him the buildings of the temple.

2 And Jesus said to them, "Do you not see all these things? Assuredly, I say to you, not one stone shall be left here upon another, that shall not be thrown down."

3 Now as He sat on the Mount of Olives, the disciples came to Him privately, saying,"Tell us, when will these things be? And what will be the sign of Your coming, and of the end of the age?"

4 And Jesus answered and said to them: "Take heed that no one deceives you.

5 For many will come in My name, saying, 'I am the Christ,' and will deceive many.

6 And you will hear of wars and rumors of wars. See that you are not troubled; for all these things must come to pass, but the end is not yet.

7 For nation will rise against nation, and kingdom against kingdom. And there will be famines, pestilences, and earthquakes in various places.

8 All these are the beginning of sorrows.

9 Then they will deliver you up to tribulation and kill you, and you will be hated by all nations for My name's sake.

10 And then many will be offended, will betray one another, and will hate one another.

11 Then many false prophets will rise up and deceive many.

12 And because lawlessness will abound, the love of many will grow cold.

13 But he who endures to the end shall be saved.

14 And this gospel of the kingdom will be preached in all the world as a witness to all the nations, and then the end will come.

15 Therefore when you see the 'abomination of desolation,' spoken of by Daniel the prophet, standing in the holy place" (whoever reads, let him understand),

16 then let those who are in Judea flee to the mountains.

17 Let him who is on the housetop not go down to take anything out of his house.

18 And let him who is in the field not go back to get his clothes.

19 But woe to those who are pregnant and to those who are nursing babies in those days!

20 And pray that your flight may not be in winter or on the Sabbath.

21 For then there will be great tribulation, such as has not been since the beginning of the world until this time, no, nor ever shall be.

22 And unless those days were shortened, no flesh would be saved; but for the elect's sake those days will be shortened.

23 Then if anyone says to you, 'Look, here is the Christ!' or 'There!' do not believe it.

24 For false christs and false prophets will rise and show great signs and wonders to deceive, if possible, even the elect.

25 See, I have told you beforehand.

26 Therefore if they say to you, 'Look, He is in the desert!' do not go out; or 'Look, He is in the inner rooms!' do not believe it.

27 For as the lightning comes from the east and flashes to the west, so also will the coming of the Son of Man be.

28 For wherever the carcass is, there the eagles will be gathered together.

29 Immediately after the tribulation of those days the sun will be darkened, and the moon will not give its light; the stars will fall from heaven, and the powers of the heavens will be shaken.

30 Then the sign of the Son of Man will appear in heaven, and then all the tribes of the earth will mourn, and they will see the Son of Man coming on the clouds of heaven with power and great glory.

31 And He will send His angels with a great sound of a trumpet, and they will gather together His elect from the four winds, from one end of heaven to the other.

32 Now learn this parable from the fig tree: When its branch has already become tender and puts forth leaves, you know that summer is near.

33 So you also, when you see all these things, know that it is near - at the doors!

34 Assuredly, I say to you, this generation will by no means pass away till all these things take place.

35 Heaven and earth will pass away, but My words will by no means pass away.

36 But of that day and hour no one knows, not even the angels of heaven, but My Father only.

37 But as the days of Noah were, so also will the coming of the Son of Man be.

38 For as in the days before the flood, they were eating and drinking, marrying and giving in marriage, until the day that Noah entered the ark,

39 and did not know until the flood came and took them all away, so also will the coming of the Son of Man be.

40 Then two men will be in the field: one will be taken and the other left.

41 Two women will be grinding at the mill: one will be taken and the other left.

42 Watch therefore, for you do not know what hour your Lord is coming.

43 But know this, that if the master of the house had known what hour the thief would come, he would have watched and not allowed his house to be broken into.

44 Therefore you also be ready, for the Son of Man is coming at an hour you do not expect.

45 Who then is a faithful and wise servant, whom his master made ruler over his household, to give them food in due season?

46 Blessed is that servant whom his master, when he comes, will find so doing.

47 Assuredly, I say to you that he will make him ruler over all his goods.

48 But if that evil servant says in his heart, 'My master is delaying his coming,'

49 and begins to beat his fellow servants, and to eat and drink with the drunkards,

50 the master of that servant will come on a day when he is not looking for him and at an hour that he is not aware of,

51 and will cut him in two and appoint him his portion with the hypocrites. There shall be weeping and gnashing of teeth.

Matthew 24

1 The Revelation of Jesus Christ, which God gave Him to show His servants - things which must shortly take place. And He sent and signified it by His angel to His servant John,

2 who bore witness to the word of God, and to the testimony of Jesus Christ, to all things that he saw.

3 Blessed is he who reads and those who hear the words of this prophecy, and keep those things which are written in it; for the time is near.

4 John, to the seven churches which are in Asia:
Grace to you and peace from Him who is and who was and who is to come, and from the seven Spirits who are before His throne,

5 and from Jesus Christ, the faithful witness, the firstborn from the dead, and the ruler over the kings of the earth.
To Him who loved us and washed us from our sins in His own blood,

6 and has made us kings and priests to His God and Father, to Him be glory and dominion forever and ever. Amen.

7 Behold, He is coming with clouds, and every eye will see Him, even they who pierced Him. And all the tribes of the earth will mourn because of Him. Even so, Amen.

8 "I am the Alpha and the Omega, the Beginning and the End," says the Lord, "who is and who was and who is to come, the Almighty."

9 I, John, both your brother and companion in the tribulation and kingdom and patience of Jesus Christ, was on the island that is called Patmos for the word of God and for the testimony of Jesus Christ.

10 I was in the Spirit on the Lord's Day, and I heard behind me a loud voice, as of a trumpet,

11 saying, "I am the Alpha and the Omega, the First and the Last," and, "What you see, write in a book and send it to the seven churches which are in Asia: to Ephesus, to Smyrna, to Pergamos, to Thyatira, to Sardis, to Philadelphia, and to Laodicea."

12 Then I turned to see the voice that spoke with me. And having turned I saw seven golden lampstands,

13 and in the midst of the seven lampstands One like the Son of Man, clothed with a garment down to the feet and girded about the chest with a golden band.

14 His head and hair were white like wool, as white as snow, and His eyes like a flame of fire;

15 His feet were like fine brass, as if refined in a furnace, and His voice as the sound of many waters;

16 He had in His right hand seven stars, out of His mouth went a sharp two-edged sword, and His countenance was like the sun shining in its strength.

17 And when I saw Him, I fell at His feet as dead. But He laid His right hand on me, saying to me, "Do not be afraid; I am the First and the Last.

18 I am He who lives, and was dead, and behold, I am alive forevermore. Amen. And I have the keys of Hades and of Death.

19 Write the things which you have seen, and the things which are, and the things which will take place after this.

20 The mystery of the seven stars which you saw in My right hand, and the seven golden lampstands: The seven stars are the angels of the seven churches, and the seven lampstands which you saw are the seven churches.
Revelation 1

1 "To the angel of the church of Ephesus write,
'These things says He who holds the seven stars in His right hand, who walks in the midst of the seven golden lampstands:

2 "I know your works, your labor, your patience, and that you cannot bear those who are evil. And you have tested those who say they are apostles and are not, and have found them liars;

3 and you have persevered and have patience, and have labored for My name's sake and have not become weary.

4 Nevertheless I have this against you, that you have left your first love.

5 Remember therefore from where you have fallen; repent and do the first works, or else I will come to you quickly and remove your lampstand from its place - unless you repent.

6 But this you have, that you hate the deeds of the Nicolaitans, which I also hate.

7 "He who has an ear, let him hear what the Spirit says to the churches. To him who overcomes I will give to eat from the tree of life, which is in the midst of the Paradise of God.'"

8 "And to the angel of the church in Smyrna write,

'These things says the First and the Last, who was dead, and came to life:

9 "I know your works, tribulation, and poverty (but you are rich); and I know the blasphemy of those who say they are Jews and are not, but are a synagogue of satan.

10 Do not fear any of those things which you are about to suffer. Indeed, the devil is about to throw some of you into prison, that you may be tested, and you will have tribulation ten days. Be faithful until death, and I will give you the crown of life.

11 "He who has an ear, let him hear what the Spirit says to the churches. He who overcomes shall not be hurt by the second death.'"

12 "And to the angel of the church in Pergamos write,

'These things says He who has the sharp two-edged sword:

13 "I know your works, and where you dwell, where satan's throne is. And you hold fast to My name, and did not deny My faith even in the days in which Antipas was My faithful martyr, who was killed among you, where satan dwells.

14 But I have a few things against you, because you have there those who hold the doctrine of Balaam, who taught Balak to put a stumbling block before the children of Israel, to eat things sacrificed to idols, and to commit sexual immorality.

15 Thus you also have those who hold the doctrine of the Nicolaitans, which thing I hate.

16 Repent, or else I will come to you quickly and will fight against them with the sword of My mouth.

17 "He who has an ear, let him hear what the Spirit says to the churches. To him who overcomes I will give some of the hidden manna to eat. And I will give him a white stone, and on the stone a new name written which no one knows except him who receives it.'"

18 "And to the angel of the church in Thyatira write,

'These things says the Son of God, who has eyes like a flame of fire, and His feet like fine brass:

19 "I know your works, love, service, faith, and your patience; and as for your works, the last are more than the first.

20 Nevertheless I have a few things against you, because you allow that woman Jezebel, who calls herself a prophetess, to teach and seduce My servants to commit sexual immorality and eat things sacrificed to idols.

21 And I gave her time to repent of her sexual immorality, and she did not repent.

22 Indeed I will cast her into a sickbed, and those who commit adultery with her into great tribulation, unless they repent of their deeds.

23 I will kill her children with death, and all the churches shall know that I am He who searches the minds and hearts. And I will give to each one of you according to your works.

24 Now to you I say, and to the rest in Thyatira, as many as do not have this

doctrine, who have not known the depths of satan, as they say, I will put on you no other burden.

25 But hold fast what you have till I come.

26 And he who overcomes, and keeps My works until the end, to him I will give power over the nations –

27 'He shall rule them with a rod of iron; They shall be dashed to pieces like the potter's vessels' – as I also have received from My Father;

28 and I will give him the morning star.

29 "He who has an ear, let him hear what the Spirit says to the churches.'"
Revelation 2

1 "And to the angel of the church in Sardis write,

'These things says He who has the seven Spirits of God and the seven stars: "I know your works, that you have a name that you are alive, but you are dead.

2 Be watchful, and strengthen the things which remain, that are ready to die, for I have not found your works perfect before God.

3 Remember therefore how you have received and heard; hold fast and repent. Therefore if you will not watch, I will come upon you as a thief, and you will not know what hour I will come upon you.

4 You have a few names even in Sardis who have not defiled their garments; and they shall walk with Me in white, for they are worthy.

5 He who overcomes shall be clothed in white garments, and I will not blot out his name from the Book of Life; but I will confess his name before My Father and before His angels.

6 "He who has an ear, let him hear what the Spirit says to the churches.'"

7 "And to the angel of the church in Philadelphia write,

'These things says He who is holy, He who is true, "He who has the key of David, He who opens and no one shuts, and shuts and no one opens":

8 "I know your works. See, I have set before you an open door, and no one can shut it; for you have a little strength, have kept My word, and have not denied My name.

9 Indeed I will make those of the synagogue of satan, who say they are Jews and are not, but lie – indeed I will make them come and worship before your feet, and to know that I have loved you.

10 Because you have kept My command to persevere, I also will keep you from the hour of trial which shall come upon the whole world, to test those who dwell on the earth.

11 Behold, I am coming quickly! Hold fast what you have, that no one may take your crown.

12 He who overcomes, I will make him a pillar in the temple of My God, and he shall go out no more. I will write on him the name of My God and the name of the city of My God, the New Jerusalem, which comes down out of heaven from My God. And I will write on him My new name.

13 "He who has an ear, let him hear what the Spirit says to the churches.'"

14 "And to the angel of the church of the Laodiceans write,

'These things says the Amen, the Faithful and True Witness, the Beginning of the creation of God:

15 "I know your works, that you are neither cold nor hot. I could wish you were cold or hot.

16 So then, because you are lukewarm, and neither cold nor hot, I will vomit you out of My mouth.

17 Because you say, 'I am rich, have become wealthy, and have need of nothing' - and do not know that you are wretched, miserable, poor, blind, and naked -

18 I counsel you to buy from Me gold refined in the fire, that you may be rich; and white garments, that you may be clothed, that the shame of your nakedness may not be revealed; and anoint your eyes with eye salve, that you may see.

19 As many as I love, I rebuke and chasten. Therefore be zealous and repent.

20 Behold, I stand at the door and knock. If anyone hears My voice and opens the door, I will come in to him and dine with him, and he with Me.

21 To him who overcomes I will grant to sit with Me on My throne, as I also over-came and sat down with My Father on His throne.

22 "He who has an ear, let him hear what the Spirit says to the churches."''"
Revelation 3

1 After these things I looked, and behold, a door standing open in heaven. And the first voice which I heard was like a trumpet speaking with me, saying, "Come up here, and I will show you things which must take place after this."

2 Immediately I was in the Spirit; and behold, a throne set in heaven, and One sat on the throne.

3 And He who sat there was like a jasper and a sardius stone in appearance; and there was a rainbow around the throne, in appearance like an emerald.

4 Around the throne were twenty-four thrones, and on the thrones I saw twenty-four elders sitting, clothed in white robes; and they had crowns of gold on their heads.

5 And from the throne proceeded lightnings, thunderings, and voices. Seven lamps of fire were burning before the throne, which are the seven Spirits of God.

6 Before the throne there was a sea of glass, like crystal. And in the midst of the throne, and around the throne, were four living creatures full of eyes in front and in back.

7 The first living creature was like a lion, the second living creature like a calf, the third living creature had a face like a man, and the fourth living creature was like a flying eagle.

8 The four living creatures, each having six wings, were full of eyes around and within. And they do not rest day or night, saying:
"Holy, holy, holy, Lord God Almighty, who was and is and is to come!"

9 Whenever the living creatures give glory and honor and thanks to Him who sits on the throne, who lives forever and ever,

10 the twenty-four elders fall down before Him who sits on the throne and worship Him who lives forever and ever, and cast their crowns before the throne, saying:

11 "You are worthy, O Lord, to receive glory and honor and power; for You created all things, and by Your will they exist and were created."
Revelation 4

1 And I saw in the right hand of Him who sat on the throne a scroll written inside and on the back, sealed with seven seals.

2 Then I saw a strong angel proclaiming with a loud voice, "Who is worthy to open the scroll and to loose its seals?"

3 And no one in heaven or on the earth or under the earth was able to open the scroll, or to look at it.

4 So I wept much, because no one was found worthy to open and read the scroll, or to look at it.

5 But one of the elders said to me, "Do not weep. Behold, the Lion of the tribe of Judah, the Root of David, has prevailed to open the scroll and to loose its seven seals."

6 And I looked, and behold, in the midst of the throne and of the four living creatures, and in the midst of the elders, stood a Lamb as though it had been slain, having seven horns and seven eyes, which are the seven Spirits of God sent out into all the earth.

7 Then He came and took the scroll out of the right hand of Him who sat on the throne.

8 Now when He had taken the scroll, the four living creatures and the twenty-four elders fell down before the Lamb, each having a harp, and golden bowls full of incense, which are the prayers of the saints.

9 And they sang a new song, saying:
"You are worthy to take the scroll, and to open its seals; for You were slain, and have redeemed us to God by Your blood out of every tribe and tongue and people and nation,

10 And have made us kings and priests to our God; and we shall reign on the earth."

11 Then I looked, and I heard the voice of many angels around the throne, the living creatures, and the elders; and the number of them was ten thousand times ten thousand, and thousands of thousands,

12 saying with a loud voice:
"Worthy is the Lamb who was slain to receive power and riches and wisdom, and strength and honor and glory and blessing!"

13 And every creature which is in heaven and on the earth and under the earth and such as are in the sea, and all that are in them, I heard saying:
"Blessing and honour and glory and power be to Him who sits on the throne, and to the Lamb, forever and ever!"

14 Then the four living creatures said, "Amen!" And the twenty-four elders fell down and worshiped Him who lives forever and ever.

Revelation 5

1 Now I saw when the Lamb opened one of the seals; and I heard one of the four living creatures saying with a voice like thunder, "Come and see."

2 And I looked, and behold, a white horse. He who sat on it had a bow; and a crown was given to him, and he went out conquering and to conquer.

3 When He opened the second seal, I heard the second living creature saying,

"Come and see."

4 Another horse, fiery red, went out. And it was granted to the one who sat on it to take peace from the earth, and that people should kill one another; and there was given to him a great sword.

5 When He opened the third seal, I heard the third living creature say, "Come and see." So I looked, and behold, a black horse, and he who sat on it had a pair of scales in his hand.

6 And I heard a voice in the midst of the four living creatures saying, "A quart of wheat for a denarius, and three quarts of barley for a denarius; and do not harm the oil and the wine."

7 When He opened the fourth seal, I heard the voice of the fourth living creature saying, "Come and see."

8 So I looked, and behold, a pale horse. And the name of him who sat on it was Death, and Hades followed with him. And power was given to them over a fourth of the earth, to kill with sword, with hunger, with death, and by the beasts of the earth.

9 When He opened the fifth seal, I saw under the altar the souls of those who had been slain for the word of God and for the testimony which they held.

10 And they cried with a loud voice, saying, "How long, O Lord, holy and true, until You judge and avenge our blood on those who dwell on the earth?"

11 Then a white robe was given to each of them; and it was said to them that they should rest a little while longer, until both the number of their fellow servants and their brethren, who would be killed as they were, was completed.

12 I looked when He opened the sixth seal, and behold, there was a great earthquake; and the sun became black as sackcloth of hair, and the moon became like blood.

13 And the stars of heaven fell to the earth, as a fig tree drops its late figs when it is shaken by a mighty wind.

14 Then the sky receded as a scroll when it is rolled up, and every mountain and island was moved out of its place.

15 And the kings of the earth, the great men, the rich men, the commanders, the mighty men, every slave and every free man, hid themselves in the caves and in the rocks of the mountains,

16 and said to the mountains and rocks, "Fall on us and hide us from the face of Him who sits on the throne and from the wrath of the Lamb!

17 For the great day of His wrath has come, and who is able to stand?"
Revelation 6

I Love you, I Love you. Time is urgent. You yourselves must prepare. You must be prepared to do all things in obedience that I ask you to. I will speak again.
Do not broadcast this Message until the appointed time. This you will know, for I will tell you. Do as I ask you. I Love you.

Saturday 30 September 1995
Children of this world, I announce to you these two Messages of Mine

to the world. They are indeed grave Words, but they are Mine. Free-masonry, you have allowed to grow around you like an ivy, and it is choking you. The evil one has ruled this world through it. You do not see through the block that he has placed in front of you.

I tell you these Words and they will be in vain, for he has coiled him-self around you so much that you do not see the danger that you are in. These Words that I release to you are for you to benefit from. If you listen to them, then you will.

You look for strange happenings to see, but I tell you that they are already happening and you do not see them. You are like the sheep without shepherds. They cannot, and will not, teach the ways that I have laid down.

I declare to the world that I am Coming in judgement, and many of you, who say that you love Me, do not. You perform your deeds in the streets at the whim of the evil one. So be it; your father is the father of lies, and you have become his sons and daughters.

These Words that I give, I ask all of you, who do love Me, to spread them to the four corners of the earth, so that all shall know them. These are My Words to the world.

Already My Angels have finished its preparation
Tuesday 29 November 1994

My children, listen to the Words that I speak this day, for you have not listened to My promptings. I have given you an order, which you only begin to carry out now. My sons, I have told you how things will be; now listen. My sign is imminent. Already My Angels have finished its preparation. I will not give you dates for it; it is not yours to know. This sign, that I speak of, will rock the world in the earlier part of your new year[1]. The world will know Me in Truth. Tell My children to seek the Truth before this time. Do not neglect your posts, little sons, but stand at them waiting. For soon you shall see all of My Words come to fruition, and you shall know. Many people, at this time of Truth, will hurl themselves headlong into the abyss, for they shall have no-one to turn to. My children will scream in fear when they see the Truth as it really is. I Bless you, My children. I Love you.

[1] *Jesus did not say which new year.*

Fire shall shoot from the sky
Saturday 11 March 1995
From the Angel Ephraim

The world is on fire, My brothers; it is on fire with the flame of hell. You, too, my sisters, must know these Words. My name is Ephraim, and I am an Angel of God sent to tell you of these things. When we come, when we are unchained, then the world will know that we are the Lord's servants sent to do His bidding. The ones of this world, who will not listen, will be cut down with the sword. There will be no mercy. You will see this in your humanness as the plagues - and many there will be. Fire shall shoot from the sky and many people will run burning, but the fire will not be put out. The smell of burning flesh will burn the nostrils of those who love God, and they will rejoice as they realise that they have run the race to the end. The great gates of hell will open for those who wish to go. There will be no peace anywhere on this earth, for we will come striking at those who do not have the signs that they need. The sky that you see now will be many colours, but not blue, but you will only see these as the fire lights up the sky - for the world will be darkened by the spirits that will roam free. You will see things, that have been kept hidden in the dark, being paraded openly in the streets. Blood will run everywhere, for it is we who gather those who are bound for the winepress of Gods Anger, and the little ones of God will walk up to their waist in blood. Many will cry out for death in this time, but there will be none, for death will be held back until they are given what they meted out. demons will over-run the holy places until we have routed them out. Desecration after desecration will take place within the Holy of Holies, and the people of God will have much to suffer as they see these things. For this is the time of the persecution of the saints of God. Brothers and sisters, they will hound you, they will try to break you down, but you will be held safe.

This Message is given solely to let you see that you must do all things urgently. There is no time, for already the Angel flies over you crying: 'Woe! and woe! to all who do not belong to the Son of God.' Take these Words and let them be the driving force behind you. Do the Master's Work, and do it well. Within a period of your time, you will have seen the very Truth, and you will finally realise the Truth and the importance of your Work that the Master has allotted to you. All fear must be cast from your hearts, for many demons attack the children of God at this time. This you will know, for it shall be shown you, in this time of truth, not all the chosen ones will be saved. Many of them have allowed pride and complacency to take over their lives. Do not worry, My brothers and sisters, but listen to the Words of our Master, Jesus, and obey in truth and obedience, for this is your protection. In doing this, you relieve the great Pain that our beautiful Saviour, Jesus, undergoes for the Love of His children. Do all things well and in truth. This is my plea to you. I leave you in the Love of our Master, Jesus. I love you, little brothers and sisters.

Toronto Blessing
Tuesday 12 September 1995

Children of Love, I call to all of you to come into this Land of Love that is in My Heart, for the wolf is snapping at your heels. He is in the midst of this world; in fact he is in this city at this time.

He has brought many henchmen with him and he prowls around looking for many souls to devour. He is here in this city to try to break you down with his evil blessing. You have succumbed to his charm.

My children, take this evil blessing from you. Go to your priests and have them pray with you, for you do not know what you are doing. Do not be deceived for many have been lost through it. They are chained to evil and this will manifest itself in their lives.

If you do not believe My Words, then watch as he breaks lives through it. he will break many priests; he will break marriages.

Look, children, the elect are falling; they are falling like raindrops. Many souls will lie like dead and rotting corpses. The birds of prey will pick their bones. Will you see what it is that I say? Will you take My Words to heart?

My sheep know Me, and I know them; they will recognise My Voice. This is My Voice calling to you to remove yourselves from the fire that already burns. Come away from the flames; do you not smell its stench? The evil one is a brigand and a thief and he comes to trick you with his lies.

I expose the Truth that his "blessing" is possession of innocent souls. It is the viper sent to bite you. It is not of My Holy Spirit. The evil one looks for many ways to take your souls and this is his plan for you.

My children, come back to Me all you who are held in bondage and chains and I will set you free. I tell you that, because of these Words, My two who are among you, will come under much attack from the evil one. They will be the victims of these Words of Truth. The penalty will be theirs, for they are the Prophets of Truth.

The eggs that the evil one has planted are now hatched. he clucks like a mother hen at his brood. These days are dark days for this world. Already My priests and My religious have fallen deep into the mire of deception. They will not look back and see that I am not in their lives. My Body is dying.

But you, My Remnant, I have come to tell you these Words and to expose the Truth of what the evil one does to you. I tell you that you must uproot this vile, evil plant from your midst. I tell you, My faithful ones, that what is called the Toronto blessing is the evil blessing of which I speak and this night I declare that it is an abomination in My sight. It mocks My Holy Spirit. Have I not told you that all who sin against the Son of Man will be forgiven but those who blaspheme against My Holy Spirit will never be forgiven?

These Words are harsh, My children, and indeed they must be. I tell you that when My people Israel were in the desert and fell ill, I gave My servant Moses the symbol for them so that they would be healed. In the same way I, Myself, was lifted up upon the Cross and I made the Eternal Sacrifice so that you would be saved. Look now to My Eucharist as I am lifted up and I will heal you of this abomination for I am indeed a God of Mercy.

But if you persist in your evil ways then I will take away what I have already given to you in Love. Do not help the evil one to destroy My Temple.

I Warn those who persist with this evil Toronto blessing.

My Little Rose, Vassula
Tuesday 27 June 1995

My children, I speak these Words through My two servants of Love and I tell you that I have listened too long to your condemnation of My Little Rose, Vassula.

She has been given to this world to speak of My Love and My Unity, but all I see when I look at you, My children, is how you judge and condemn her. You look to find her sins. Have I not said, *"Let him who is without sin cast the first stone"*? I tell you that you have cast many stones.

I ask, are you without sin? Look and see what you do. It is I that you condemn.

The Words of life that I speak through My little one you will not take. You do not recognise My Voice and I speak to you who say that you know Me - My cardinals, bishops, priests, religious and laity alike. I speak to all of you, who have sat upon the seat of judgement and condemned My Little Rose. You have not accepted the sweet, fragrant aroma of My Words that I speak through her. You have judged yourselves.

Have I not already said, *"Judge not and you will not be judged"*? So be it, children, what you have sown in your judgement, now you shall reap. I have also said, in My Revelations to the world, that whatever is taken away or added to My Word that the same will be done unto you. Many lies have been added to My Words and much you have taken away.

You condemn Me for you know it is the Truth that I speak. All I have wanted to give you is Love, but you will not accept it. You would rather listen to the calls of the evil one. I tell you, children, listen now; My Love and My Forgiveness will touch you, even at this late hour. I Love you, please listen.

Patricia of Surbiton
Sunday 17 September 1995

I will speak about My daughter, Patricia, My children. There are many in this world that will condemn even when I, their Master, have told them that they have no right. They who condemn outright My little daughter, have walked a lonely road and I have much to judge them. I declare to the world this day, that My child of innocence will do My Work until I call her. She is beloved of Me. Look deeply at the Words that I speak through her and you will find much consolation in your lives.

Retrieve the things that I have given her and that you have been told to throw away. Believe that only those who flounder in their own mission would tell these lies of her. They, who condemn her, are caught in a web of pride. Their pride is the self that they will not die to. Their pride will judge them.

Woe to you who condemn My Messengers, for you shall crawl upon your belly with the one who sent you, for condemnation is his food and it shall be yours too. Your father is the father of lies and the deceiver, for if God were your Father you would obey Him, but since He is not, then you do not know how to obey.

My daughter is Mine. She is beloved of Mine. I Love her.

Tom Lennon
Tuesday 10 October 1995

My children, those who condemn the Prophets that I send, I will condemn them before My Father in Heaven. It would be better that they had a millstone tied around their necks and thrown into the deepest part of the ocean.

I speak to the world about those who condemn My little ones.

You are hypocrites, whitewashed walls and you will soon fall in your greed. You, who purport to be My servants, you have led My people astray in your greed. Money has become your god. What you call visions, now are imaginings. Your visions fail you because of your greed and your pride.

The pain that you feel is your own and not Mine, nor My Mother's. You were once true, and now you are not, but you will be again. Soon you shall fall, but you shall rise in humility and soon, within a time, you shall know My Words.

I am drawing My people away from you for your falseness and you shall draw yourself into debt and you shall fall for the allotted time. You shall bear the yoke of humility but you shall condemn no more.

My son, Thomas, I declare to the world, is My Prophet for these times. Do not believe the lies that you have been told, for you have been told many from the same source.

Many who follow Me do not truly follow Me
Friday 13 February 2004

Patrick:

Jesus, You say things are going to happen soon. Many of us thought that all would have been over and done by the year 2000 but still You are saying these things will happen soon.

What is soon, Jesus? I am not asking You for a date but I am curious. I know many people that thought these things would happen before the year 2000 no longer believe in the Words that both You and Your Mother speak through Your Prophets and Visionaries and Seers. What is happening?

Jesus:

My son, it is good that you ask these questions. As I have said before, many who follow Me do not truly follow Me but they only follow the Words that are sensational and they look for sensational events. When these events, that they thought would happen, did not, in their eyes, they became tired and moved on deeper into the world for they did not truly follow Me in the first place. My children, presume many things for they interpret My Words to suit their own desires.

I tell you many things have taken place but My children have failed to recognise them. Remember, I have said, it is not the learned and wise that will understand but those who think as children: a child believes its parents. A learned and wise person disputes what they hear for they believe that their own knowledge is greater. So, as you see, those who believed they understood what I was saying, left when their interpretation did not come to pass.

To understand My Words, that person must first begin to die to themselves; the more you die to yourself the more I can fill you with spiritual knowledge for, while self remains, it fights against that that is spiritual.

In order for Me to speak within My children they must leave this world and its ways behind for My Ways are far above this world for they are the Ways of Love. I Love you. Understand that time matters little; all will be fulfilled at the appointed time. I will say this: time grows very short and many will not listen for they have become so blinded by this world and its ways that there is no return.

Look around you, as you can read the seasons so also should you be able to read the signs of your times. In order to do this, you must read the Words that I have spoken through My Scriptures, My Mother and My Prophets and all shall become clear to those who are willing to see the Truth. Be childlike and all shall become clear.

Thank you, My son, for once again taking up your pen. I Love you.
Patrick:
Thank You, Jesus. I love You.

I Weep Tears of sadness
Wednesday 10 March 2004

My little children, as you read these, My Words, hear Me as I Weep Tears of sadness. My Tears are for you who read these Words. I Weep for the world and you are a part of it. I Weep for the things you will read here; knowing them to be the very Truth, and you will not carry them out.

But still, My child, I call you, I encourage you to at least carry out some of what I ask and to encourage others to do the same. If you look in truth for the treasure that lies here then you will find it, you will know Me.

I Love you. Let My Tears turn to joy in you.

Wake up and see the Truth
Wednesday 10 March 2004

Jesus:

My child, I Love you and I come in these Words to tell you that My Coming is soon. I speak these Words to each of My children as if they stood before Me with arms outstretched.

Now is the time to listen for in not many days time, many things will begin to change upon this earth. Belief in Me will become unrecognisable as what I have lain down upon this earth. Man has allowed lucifer so much freedom that he prepares now to make his greatest move against My Church and when he does, children, not many shall recognise it. For all are so consumed by self and materialism that there are very few now left who can see My Truth.

Understand, My child, as you read these Words, the danger that you are now in. This world that you live in is but a passing of time; you will not live forever for there is only Life Eternal in My Kingdom and this is what you should be preparing for. Very soon, all that you see and believe in shall be no more. The realisation of good and evil will come as a great shock to the peoples of this earth.

I say, wake up and see the Truth of what I am saying. Wake up, and understand the truth of the danger that you are in. Not many days, My child, until I return. Will you be ready for the Bridegroom? Will you have stored up oil for your lamps or shall you be like the foolish virgins?

lucifer plans to take control of My Church, he has prepared the way well with eastern spiritualism, feminism, freedom of speech, of obscenities, pornography, lies, untruth from within the walls of My Church, materialism and the greatest of all is fear. These are but a few of the ploys that he has used against My Church.

Look at the scandals within My Church, where do you think these came from? From men who listened to the lies and temptations of lucifer. If you do not believe in sin, then obviously there is no harm in fulfilling your desires.

Look, look and see the lies of lucifer at work. he causes My servants to fall and then he stands them up before this world so that My Church is torn apart by ridicule and lies. Many of My servants have become unapproachable to their flocks for they have become kings, controllers, and they use My Temple as their castles.

Do you not realise what is happening? Can you not see what lucifer is doing? Look around you! All is in turmoil. You murder your children before they are born; you feed your children with the lies of lucifer through your televisions; sex, lust, pornography, homosexuality, greed, adultery. satanism and all sorts of perversions are fed through your televisions that you sit in front of and worship for endless hours at a time.

I tell you, My children, never before, no, not even from the beginning of time, has evil been allowed to roam so freely upon this earth. I tell you, not even in the time of Noah was man so barbaric. Truly I tell you, you gather your own punishment; a punishment that has been created by your own hands. Only the just shall be left upon this earth; you shall have no need for greed for there will be very few left upon this earth and all shall be willing to help and love one another. They shall be the ones who shall have witnessed the great and terrible day of Yahweh.

You are but fooling yourselves, My children, for you do not know the day or the hour of your own deaths, yet, the way that you live is as though you were going to live for ever. I say again, wake up and realise the truth of your lives! Wake up and see what you are doing! Repent of your sinful ways and come back to My Ways. Walk with Me and, We, together, shall bring many out of the darkness for I have no hands but your hands, no feet but your feet, no lips but your lips. Wake up and begin to wage war against this war that lucifer has launched upon mankind.

My servants, (bishops, priests, brothers, nuns) I call you out of your complacency. I call you back to My Ways. I call you to look at your lives and see what you have done. Repent, I say, and let My children know the Truth, know the danger that they are in. Do not be afraid to speak of sin, of the great untruth that attacks My Church.

Remember, this is why I was Crucified for I announced to the world the lies that was within My Father's Temple. You, too, are like the Scribes and Pharisees: you sit in your comforts, your materialism and allow My children to fall into the depths of sin so that you do not have to uncover your own sin. 'Wake up,' I say!

I muster you to battle. Come fall in behind and take your places with your brothers and sisters that are not afraid to speak out and let this world know the darkness that it is in, the danger. Do not be afraid, My sons and My daughters, for I am with you, ready to wage the battle for you. Come, come I say, join Me for your reward shall be great. Long enough have you lain down and allowed the vipers to hold you. I am Jesus, the Son of the Living God, and I say I Love you.

Patrick:

I felt Jesus telling me that within the walls of the Church there was still a remnant of priests, bishops, nuns and brothers who were willing to stand up for the Truth, who were willing to be persecuted for Love of Jesus. The voices are not loud at this time but soon their cries would be heard in the streets.

I felt Him telling me, within my heart, that these were the ones who have remained loyal to the teachings of the Holy Roman Catholic Church and John Paul, our spiritual leader upon this earth. I felt also that Jesus was asking for many prayers to help those who have fallen into the traps of lucifer to break free and also, prayers for those bishops, priests, brothers and nuns who were waging the war against the evil upon this earth for many are struggling for they stand alone like voices in the wilderness. The more we pray and sacrifice, the more strength they will be given to overcome all that lucifer places before them. And, most especially, we need to pray for our Holy Father, John Paul, for he suffers much at this time.

We must remember that he sees all that is going on within the Church and has to bear the pain of all within his heart. We are on the outskirts, we see what is happening on the fringes. The things like inclusive language, the changing of Scripture, the wiping away of the Sacraments, feminism, homosexuality, but he sees much more than we could bear. So we must pray and sacrifice much so that he will be strengthened to uphold the Truth for Jesus.

Thank You, Jesus. I love You.

I need your help
Saturday 16 October 2004

I, Jesus, speak with all My children who have come here to listen to My Words. I need your help. Many do not heed these Words because of pride and because they are caught up in the world; they are too afraid to leave it behind.

I wish to send My sons to many places to do the vital Work that I have set them. This Work involves many things that will prevent many things that await their time to happen. I call on you to help them, to become involved with the setting up of My Houses. They cannot do My Work because there are not enough hands to help them. I have already spoken of a House in France that I must set up. The importance of this is significant because of what happens in the world. If you look deeply into My Words you will see the importance of this and you will know why I call for your help. There is one House that I must still keep secret. Respect My wishes in this.

Ah, the sun is setting, My children, and soon will begin the agony of what is to come. I place much emphasis on My Houses for they will be vital when the darkness begins, when My Pope is usurped. These Houses must be in place and ready for that time for they will be stepping stones, not only for the future but for now.

Come to My Heart, children, fight against the evil of the world. Forgive and forget the world and come follow Me. They will hate you and they are speaking of you in secret, in fact as you hear My Words. But do not forget, they did it to Me first. Look to these Words: they are a Warning to you.

Friday 2 July 2004

Children of this world, I call you to be watchful and save yourselves from the false promises of the evil one. I tell you this so that you can know what is coming. Many things are about to happen in what is now called Europe. The influence of the evil one in this new country is greater than you could ever know. Things that will come will seem insignificant to begin with but, as with the Jews not so long ago, the true horrors will soon emerge. Remember, what you elect now will have serious consequences although it will seem tame at the time.

Remember, too, that what is written on paper can be changed so what you think you vote for may not necessarily turn out to be. It will seem good but it will turn out the opposite.

Soon, a court will decide how and when you will worship Me; soon you will be laughed at and tortured because you follow Me. In fact they will take you to court for loving Me. A judge will preside and decide what prayers will be said in My churches and My priests will have to follow these rules.

Prayers, My children, will become empty words that mean nothing and My people will meet in underground places to worship Me. There will be two churches: one that is open and prays to itself and the other that is My True Church that worships Me in secret.

You will be aghast at these Words but I give you the Truth; already it has begun, already the wolf is at the door.

I have asked the world to reacquaint itself with the Messages of Garabandal, La Salette and I include Mount Melleray (Ireland) so that it could see the Truth of these Words and how they are being fulfilled before its eyes. Doubt not these Words, children, for you risk your soul if you do.

Read My Word Matthew 24 and find its meaning through these Words.

I Love you, children, be Warned.

1 Then Jesus went out and departed from the temple, and His disciples came up to show Him the buildings of the temple.

2 And Jesus said to them, "Do you not see all these things? Assuredly, I say to you, not one stone shall be left here upon another, that shall not be thrown

down."

3 Now as He sat on the Mount of Olives, the disciples came to Him privately, saying, "Tell us, when will these things be? And what will be the sign of Your coming, and of the end of the age?"

4 And Jesus answered and said to them: "Take heed that no one deceives you.

5 For many will come in My name, saying, 'I am the Christ,' and will deceive many.

6 And you will hear of wars and rumors of wars. See that you are not troubled; for all these things must come to pass, but the end is not yet.

7 For nation will rise against nation, and kingdom against kingdom. And there will be famines, pestilences, and earthquakes in various places.

8 All these are the beginning of sorrows.

9 "Then they will deliver you up to tribulation and kill you, and you will be hated by all nations for My name's sake.

10 And then many will be offended, will betray one another, and will hate one another.

11 Then many false prophets will rise up and deceive many.

12 And because lawlessness will abound, the love of many will grow cold.

13 But he who endures to the end shall be saved.

14 And this gospel of the kingdom will be preached in all the world as a witness to all the nations, and then the end will come.

15 Therefore when you see the 'abomination of desolation,' spoken of by Daniel the prophet, standing in the holy place" (whoever reads, let him understand),

16 then let those who are in Judea flee to the mountains.

17 Let him who is on the housetop not go down to take anything out of his house.

18 And let him who is in the field not go back to get his clothes.

19 But woe to those who are pregnant and to those who are nursing babies in those days!

20 And pray that your flight may not be in winter or on the Sabbath.

21 For then there will be great tribulation, such as has not been since the beginning of the world until this time, no, nor ever shall be.

22 And unless those days were shortened, no flesh would be saved; but for the elect's sake those days will be shortened.

23 Then if anyone says to you, 'Look, here is the Christ!' or 'There!' do not believe it.

24 For false christs and false prophets will rise and show great signs and wonders to deceive, if possible, even the elect.

25 See, I have told you beforehand.

26 Therefore if they say to you, 'Look, He is in the desert!' do not go out; or 'Look, He is in the inner rooms!' do not believe it.

27 For as the lightning comes from the east and flashes to the west, so also will the coming of the Son of Man be.

28 For wherever the carcass is, there the eagles will be gathered together.

29 Immediately after the tribulation of those days the sun will be darkened, and the moon will not give its light; the stars will fall from heaven, and the powers of

the heavens will be shaken.

30 Then the sign of the Son of Man will appear in heaven, and then all the tribes of the earth will mourn, and they will see the Son of Man coming on the clouds of heaven with power and great glory.

31 And He will send His angels with a great sound of a trumpet, and they will gather together His elect from the four winds, from one end of heaven to the other.

32 Now learn this parable from the fig tree: When its branch has already become tender and puts forth leaves, you know that summer is near.

33 So you also, when you see all these things, know that it is near – at the doors!

34 Assuredly, I say to you, this generation will by no means pass away till all these things take place.

35 Heaven and earth will pass away, but My words will by no means pass away.

36 But of that day and hour no one knows, not even the angels of heaven, but My Father only.

37 But as the days of Noah were, so also will the coming of the Son of Man be.

38 For as in the days before the flood, they were eating and drinking, marrying and giving in marriage, until the day that Noah entered the ark,

39 and did not know until the flood came and took them all away, so also will the coming of the Son of Man be.

40 Then two men will be in the field: one will be taken and the other left.

41 Two women will be grinding at the mill: one will be taken and the other left.

42 Watch therefore, for you do not know what hour your Lord is coming.

43 But know this, that if the master of the house had known what hour the thief would come, he would have watched and not allowed his house to be broken into.

44 Therefore you also be ready, for the Son of Man is coming at an hour you do not expect.

45 Who then is a faithful and wise servant, whom his master made ruler over his household, to give them food in due season?

46 Blessed is that servant whom his master, when he comes, will find so doing.

47 Assuredly, I say to you that he will make him ruler over all his goods.

48 But if that evil servant says in his heart, 'My master is delaying his coming,'

49 and begins to beat his fellow servants, and to eat and drink with the drunkards,

50 the master of that servant will come on a day when he is not looking for him and at an hour that he is not aware of,

51 and will cut him in two and appoint him his portion with the hypocrites. There shall be weeping and gnashing of teeth.

Matthew 24

The evil one has gained much ground. If I am to gain it back from him then I need your help.

Do not run from Me, do not hide from Me. The darkness grows and I give you oil for your lamp in these Words. Be My refuge, children in

90

these times. And I am with you through it all.

Look into your hearts and forgive all that holds you in bondage to the evil one. There is no time left to hold grudges.

I look at you now, I look at your hearts and your souls and I appeal to you to help Me. Come to Me. I need you.

They have been told a different doctrine
Wednesday 27 October 2004

Patrick:

Jesus, would You like to speak?

Jesus:

Yes, My servant, I would like to speak. Promote My Heart in your lives for it is dying. Those who dedicate themselves to Me in this Way are few. My Heart's infinite Treasures are the source of all Love in this world. It is a Love that no man can fathom while he lives on this earth. See how I have called you in the night to explain at least some of the Treasures in My Heart. I call all of My children to blow the dust from their hearts to allow My Divine Heart to touch theirs. Remember its Promises, remember its Love.

Many within this world do not know the true way to Me for they have been told a different doctrine. My Love is not a way of allowing you to commit sin but a way of calling you away from sin. Many today speak of My Love as a thing that allows them to do as they please but, I tell you, that it is not. In My Love, there is much work to be done.

The first part of that work is for you to begin to die to yourself. Make your body and your mind do without the sin in your life; without the things of this world. Then you will begin to know My Love in an intimate way. How can you love Me and still commit sin in your lives? How can you say that you follow Me when you do not allow Me to Love you intimately. When you begin to make your body do without a sin, it protests loudly. It tells you that you cannot do without the sin and many spirits rush to your side to try to keep you with them through that sin. The work in this is that you persevere so that when you have control over that sin, I can place the same measure of intimacy within you. If you do not stay in this intimacy, then the sin will again take control of your life.

As you die to yourself in this way, incorporate works of mercy in your lives. Forgive those who have wronged you without the justification of the world. Forgive deeply, for I have Forgiven you deeply. Remember not the sin of another but when you do, forgive immediately. Hold nothing for, if you do, it will be held against you.

Love your enemies; do good to those who persecute you and love each person that you meet. Treat them as though it were Me. Listen not to the world's way for those who tell you that this Way is wrong are those who are thieves who only loves the thief he keeps company with.

Go to those who are in sin, where they sin and befriend them and, through your works of mercy and selflessness they will come to know Me in the same way that you have.

This is the Work of My Love. I have called for Houses of Prayer to be set up and you are slow to do this, My children, because you lack dying to self. I need many people to come to Me in this Way of My Sacred Heart, to work unselfishly for My Kingdom. Those who do not wish to know are those who wish not to work to bring others to My Side; they only wish to keep all things for themselves.

Prayer too, is important in your lives. Pray always. If a child of Mine is starving and it is your prayer time what do you do? You feed My child first and then come to Me in prayer. Do you not know that I am with you intimately when you do My Work? Pray and talk to Me then too.

I am the Lord and I come to you in these Words to show you how you get caught up in the things of this world and you lose Me in the process. I Love you. Do not sit back but form many groups that will bring My Way into the world. Come to My Houses of Prayer; help Me to build them, set them up and then wear My Habit so that the world will see Me and not you. You cannot promise them anything but I can for I am God. I need you, come to Me. The Master has need of this.

IMPORTANT
RECENT
MESSAGES

By the time it comes, millions more will be lost to Me
Monday 20 December 2004

Patrick:

Jesus, would You like to speak?

Jesus:

Yes, My servant, I would like to speak. The need for My Houses to be established grows daily. They are the places which should be growing in holiness on a daily basis as the evil in the world grows also. I ask for these Houses as places of holiness to counteract the growing evil. Much of Europe is lost to Me and I must break fresh ground. My people must help you in this.

There is a growing threat to all of the places that I have established over many thousands of years. I need people with hearts that are true to bring My Truth to this world. Many turn away from Me because of the false words that are spoken about Me.

Do not doubt these things that I tell you for you do so at your peril. These are Words given to you to bring you out of your complacency, to give you a way through the tumult that approaches.

You wait for the Day of My Birth, My children, but I tell you that by the time it comes, millions more will be lost to Me. Your own children grow up without Me for you have taught them to live in the world. Will they be lost because of your complacency?

I am calling you, My children, to help Me. Help Me to save My children and your brothers and sisters from the fires of hell.

What do you do with My Words when you read them? Do they gather dust?

Read these Words, already spoken:

1 Then some Pharisees and teachers of the law came to Jesus from Jerusalem and asked,

2 "Why do your disciples break the tradition of the elders? They don't wash their hands before they eat!"

3 Jesus replied, "And why do you break the command of God for the sake of your tradition?

4 For God said, 'Honour your father and mother' and 'Anyone who curses his father or mother must be put to death.'

5 But you say that if a man says to his father or mother, 'Whatever help you might otherwise have received from me is a gift devoted to God,'

6 he is not to 'honour his father' with it. Thus you nullify the word of God for the sake of your tradition.

7 You hypocrites! Isaiah was right when he prophesied about you:

8 "'These people honour me with their lips, but their hearts are far from me.

9 They worship me in vain; their teachings are but rules taught by men.'"

10 Jesus called the crowd to him and said, "Listen and understand.

11 What goes into a man's mouth does not make him 'unclean,' but what comes out of his mouth, that is what makes him 'unclean.'"

12 Then the disciples came to him and asked, "Do you know that the Pharisees were offended when they heard this?"

13 He replied, "Every plant that my heavenly Father has not planted will be pulled up by the roots.

14 Leave them; they are blind guides. If a blind man leads a blind man, both will fall into a pit."

15 Peter said, "Explain the parable to us."

16 "Are you still so dull?" Jesus asked them.

17 "Don't you see that whatever enters the mouth goes into the stomach and then out of the body?

18 But the things that come out of the mouth come from the heart, and these make a man 'unclean.'

19 For out of the heart come evil thoughts, murder, adultery, sexual immorality, theft, false testimony, slander.

20 These are what make a man 'unclean'; but eating with unwashed hands does not make him 'unclean.'"

21 Leaving that place, Jesus withdrew to the region of Tyre and Sidon.

22 A Canaanite woman from that vicinity came to him, crying out, "Lord, Son of David, have mercy on me! My daughter is suffering terribly from demon-possession."

23 Jesus did not answer a word. So his disciples came to him and urged him, "Send her away, for she keeps crying out after us."

24 He answered, "I was sent only to the lost sheep of Israel."

25 The woman came and knelt before him. "Lord, help me!" she said.

26 He replied, "It is not right to take the children's bread and toss it to their dogs."

27 "Yes, Lord," she said, "but even the dogs eat the crumbs that fall from their masters' table."

28 Then Jesus answered, "Woman, you have great faith! Your request is granted." And her daughter was healed from that very hour.

29 Jesus left there and went along the Sea of Galilee. Then he went up on a mountainside and sat down.

30 Great crowds came to him, bringing the lame, the blind, the crippled, the mute and many others, and laid them at his feet; and he healed them.

31 The people were amazed when they saw the mute speaking, the crippled made well, the lame walking and the blind seeing. And they praised the God of Israel.

32 Jesus called his disciples to him and said, "I have compassion for these people; they have already been with me three days and have nothing to eat. I do not want to send them away hungry, or they may collapse on the way."

33 His disciples answered, "Where could we get enough bread in this remote place to feed such a crowd?"

34 "How many loaves do you have?" Jesus asked.

"Seven," they replied, "and a few small fish."

35 He told the crowd to sit down on the ground.

36 Then he took the seven loaves and the fish, and when he had given thanks, he broke them and gave them to the disciples, and they in turn to the people.

37 They all ate and were satisfied. Afterward the disciples picked up seven basketfuls of broken pieces that were left over.

38 The number of those who ate was four thousand, besides women and children.

39 After Jesus had sent the crowd away, he got into the boat and went to the vicinity of Magadan. Matthew 15

Listen for Me at all times
Monday 20 December 2004

Patrick:

Jesus, I love You. I really love You, although You would not think it many times. Thank You for everything and may Your Birthday be a happy one.

Jesus:

My little son, I Love you. It brings joy to My Heart in this time of loneliness when you speak to Me in these words. Very few recognise that this is the time of My Birth. Very few celebrate the time of My Birth rather, they celebrate the world. They rejoice in sin instead of Holiness.

I waited long for you, My son, to come to Me. I ask that you begin to spend more time with Me. Listen for Me at all times, both day and night. Keep your book with you at all times and be prepared to give Me a Voice when I call.

I Love you, My son, and I say again the loneliness of My Heart is great. I am a God that has been rejected by His subjects. I am a redundant God to this generation. Believe Me when I say, all Heaven is silent and they wait for the moment when I will say, enough. On that day the earth will shake, it will convulse and much devastation will reign. Mankind does not realise in its blindness what they are doing. They do not realise, as I created the earth, I can also destroy it.

If something is unclean what do you do? You cleanse and renew it. Alas, the time is coming when no longer will I allow the blasphemy to continue.

Do not forget Me, My son, at this time I need your love. Allow Me to be with you to celebrate My Birth. Allow Me in Love, son, to enjoy this time within your heart. I Love you.

My Army of Little Souls...have not yet developed
Tuesday 21 December 2004

Patrick:

Another day and I feel called by the Master to sit at His Feet and be taught by Him. His Life is my life and I must be open to Him when He calls.

There is no life other than that that He has called me to. My life lives within the framework of what He has called me to. If I go outside of that framework then I am in sin, I am no longer part of the fabric that He is weaving in me.

I do not feel Him, I feel just the call to write these Words. It is not the night, which He usually calls me in. As the time of His Birth approaches, I feel more and more His sadness. It seems that many, many souls are being taken from Him. How, I do not know but it seems to be the falsities that are being taught by unscrupulous priests and people.

How do I convey the sadness of this God that I feel within me? How do I tell those who read this what He allows me to feel in this moment that He bids me write? It is not easy to describe an Agony that does not exist in human terms. His Agony is Love, I hear Him say, a Love for which He has given everything and would give yet more even to those who betray Him most. He tells me that He is the Good Shepherd who lays down His Life for His sheep. He is the God who stoops so low to His created and bows His Head in Agony and submission to His created; for Love of them.

And yet, we, the created, deny in our daily lives that Love that is given so unselfishly.

I wait for Him to give me the Words that I need to continue writing. I love Him with all my being. There is nothing more to give. But, no, I hear Him say, there is more, more than a man could believe that he could give. If we but allow Him to take us along the road that He wishes to take us, then He will show us just how much we can give.

Through sin, we have moved away from Him and we do not know how to proceed on this path that He takes us on. He wishes to show us.

Jesus:

I will take you upon the Path of Love, My child, if you but allow Me through these Words of Love that I give you. I emphasise again, the Words already spoken by Me.

You stand before a door. That door leads to the path upon which I shall take you to Me. The key is in your hand. The key is you. You must fashion the key, mould it into the shape of the lock that is in the door. You begin by looking into your life at the sin that is there. You are given scales to weigh up the difference between your love of sin and your love of Me. If your love for Me is found wanting then the sin will outweigh it and the shape of your key will not fit the door. It can only fit in one door; the door to hell.

If you have a desire within you to rid yourself of sin then I can help you reshape the key, I will give you the tools to do so. These tools are: a sorrow for your sin and Love.

Love is the shaper of all things. If there is love for Me in your heart then you will begin not to want to sin. As sin diminishes by this method, it will be replaced by Love, My Love. Love will compel you not to sin and, if allowed, will lead you to shape the key to fit the lock of the door behind which I stand.

I do not say that it will be easy. No, there is a battle ahead for you must fight to the death that which controls you; namely sin. Each time you fall into sin, you become more and more embroiled in it. The more you overcome sin, the more shaped by Love you are. To fight, to overcome that which you are overcome by, is the essence of the key, that you hold in your hand.

You will not go unaided, no. I will send you Grace as a sheild against the flaming arrows of temptation from the evil one. All you need to do is to stay away from those situations that lead you into sin. You know your sin, you know where you fall away from Me. You must stay away from it. The evil one knows your weakness but I know it too. I can strengthen your weakness; I can make you strong where you are weak. Listen to My Voice; listen to Me as I call you, in the Graces given, away from that which takes you from Me.

The greatest sin of man and, I say woman, is sex. It is the most subtle. Sex is given for an expression of love and creation. It is a power given. Many only misuse that power in this progressing world, progressing away from Me. Those who say that it does not touch them are liars for it touches all in some degree.

Self is the inheritance of Eden and sin its cohort, that is why it must be died to. Self is what gives in to sin. Know what leads you into sin and you can avoid it.

Patrick:

Jesus, I thank You for such powerful Words. I know these things within my heart but I do not always do them. Sin is powerful, it seems to overcome when we least expect it.

Jesus:

It is because you allow it to overcome you and you forget one thing: I am more powerful than sin; I have overcome it. I have taken on all sin and I have given you ways to overcome it, you must use these in order to overcome it fully. The power of sin is indeed great because you give it the power by not dying to the self, the part of you that wants to do it.

Patrick:

So, Jesus, it is what I have already given in to in my sin that is the most powerful part. But You are telling me that I can take the power back from the evil one by dying to my self. I can overcome because You have first overcome it.

Jesus:

To follow Me, you must throw off the shackles of sin, that that keeps you away from Me. Temptations are powerful and become more so as the soul battles with self but that is only because the soul thinks that he cannot overcome it. The evil one has fed him lies to keep him a prisoner. I only give the Truth and the Truth is more powerful than lies.

Let your love of Me be the birth of the new man within you. See what I have done for you and continue the fight at all times, if you do not, then the evil one will devour you. If you love Me then you will follow Me.

Patrick:

Jesus, You are indeed the Good Shepherd. I feel by Your Words that You are looking after us all and all we have to do is do it; become new by knowing that we do not have to give in to the lies of lucifer. We fail so many times but we know that because of Your Death on the Cross, we are Forgiven. But that is no excuse to carry on sinning. I love You, Jesus, because You are so Good.

Jesus:

I Love you, My servant, and there is a vast treasure within My Heart that I wish to give to you. Come, come inside My Heart for it is an open door to you. It is yours by birthright. On the day that the sacred water was poured upon your head, you became Mine. I had to run after you like an unruly dog but you would not come to Me as all My children do. Place here the Words of the prologue of My Life for they tell powerfully what I wish to say to those who would stand before the door that leads to Me. They are the Words of Love and they are like an oath that tells what I would do for My lost ones.

Prologue Song of the Carpenter Book Three

The father waited for his daughter. She had gone out with her friends and had not come home. He leaned painfully closer to the fire and began to stir the pot of stew that hung over it. It was for her supper. It had been many years since he last saw her but he had cooked the meal each evening, hoping she would come. Each morning he threw it out.

This time, he had gone out himself to look for the ingredients of the meal for his servants had been sent out to look for her. They had brought back tales of the sightings of her in various places and his heart had stirred with love. He knew what she liked and wanted to give it to her, wanted her to know that by doing it, he loved her. He had searched high and low for the herbs and spices that were particular to her taste. He had cooked it for her but she had not returned. It was already morning and he would throw it out again. He stirred the pot and his heart grasped the last few moments of hope before he would carry the steaming pot outside into the half light of the morning and pour it out. Wild animals would eat it greedily.

It was not that she did not like the life that she led with him. He had adorned her with precious jewels; bangles and bracelets for her arms and ankles, a crown for her head that had more diamonds than any kings, rings for her nose that would enhance her beauty. All made of the finest gold that he could find. He sent her robes of finespun material decorated with handsome embroidery to embellish her flawless skin. He had spoken love-words to her and wooed her as a bride. But she wanted that, and her friends. The man sighed.

She had become their whore. She slept with anyone who asked her and worshipped their gods of stone that stood silent and cold while they were invoked with impassioned pleas. He had begged her not to do it for they gave her nothing but still she worshipped them even though she did not need them for he had given her everything that her heart desired.

The man sighed again. He seemed to spend his life sighing.

In the years that he had waited for her to return, he had sent many servants to her with words that might bring her back. He offered her more of the precious jewels and she took them but she did not return. He had sent his own soldiers to help her fight her battles when her whoring got her into trouble with her lovers and, for a while, it looked as though she would come home. But she did not.

He searched for the most eloquent envoys and sent them to her. He sent words of love, of anger, of promises, of entreaties but to no avail. He had chosen her, from all of his daughters, to be his Queen but she had rejected him. The servants that he sent she had beaten them and some she even killed, saying that she did not recognise his voice in them. He could not understand her ways.

When she was young, when her breasts were budding into womanhood, he had chosen her. She had gazed with adoring eyes at him and hung on to his every word. Even though her sisters were older than her she would reign, hold the throne of all the earth and she would be the apple of her father's eye. But her eyes were coy and she did not always look at him. They sought the strangers and foreigners that came to pay homage to him. She walked with them and gave herself to them and they knew her as a wife, as a whore. She dangled her jewels before them and sent for them to join her in her bed for she had riches beyond compare and they wanted them. He had tried to bargain with her, to make her change her mind so that she would come back to him. She shattered his heart with her refusals.

The man wiped the tears from his eyes.

Patrick:

Oh, Jesus, this seems a very sad story but looking at it through my own life, I know that it is true.

I can feel You urging not to go back down the path and away from the door. I feel you urging me to continue fighting against the self that is in me. I can see that by allowing your Words to put me down because of their Truth, I can, easily, walk away from You. But if I take them as great encouragement, then they are the Graces that You have spoken of. If I allow them to, by dying to self, then I know that You want me to return to You, even though I am a sinner. My God, I love You.

Jesus:
I would speak again of My Army of Little Souls for they have not yet developed. Many are afraid to go on this path that I call them upon but, I tell you, it is a very powerful path. A distinguished few have travelled it. I name but one: My Little Flower, My Therese. Look at her life. Was this not a powerful witness to My Little Army. Did she not hold My Head in her arms and love Me, despite it all? Was her heart not inflamed with My Love? Was not her Little Way not a Treasure of My Heart and a way in which to find Me?

My little Flower responded to the sunlight that I gave to her because she saw through the wiles of lucifer. She called out to Me and I answered her and I gave her this Little Way because it has been in the hearts of many. She brought forth the Little Army of My Love.

There are many more that I wish to call to live in this Way. Where are you whom I have called in your heart? Why do you not answer Me when I call? Has the world caught you in its snares? Then break free of them for My sake and come, follow Me through this door that you stand outside. Why do you hesitate?

Ask My daughter, Mary, to paint the picture that I give to you and make it part of the other images that I give to you and in this way will many realise what it is that I call them to. This Little Army of Love will help Me bring many souls to My side.

Patrick:
Thank You for this, Jesus. I believe within my heart that this is another treasure of Your Most Sacred Heart. How could we refuse such powerful help? Without You, I am nothing. Without You, the world is nothing.

Jesus:
I am the Alpha and the Omega, I am the Beginning and the End. All that is not within this does not exist. I am Everything. They will say of you, too, that you made up all of these things and that spirits rule you but, remember, they said it of Me too. They said that I cast out beelzebub by beelzebub and they beat Me for it just as they will beat your spirit for it. Remember these things.

I give you a prayer for My Little Army of Souls:

Jesus, All-Powerful God,
I give You my life.
I pour it into Your Hands
As a libation of Love.
Help me, by the merits
Of Your Most Sacred Heart,
To love, to give, to sacrifice, to penetrate
Your Pain
With my little love.
Give me the Graces needed

To love You and to follow You
In Truth, in Love, in Obedience
And to offer to You
Everything
So that Your Graces can flow into
The hearts of many.
May my heart and soul
Mirror your Abundant Heart.
I love You.
Most Powerful Jesus,
Help me to avoid all occasions of sin
For Your Greater Glory.
I ask nothing but Your Glory.

Patrick:

What can I say, Jesus? Grace on top of Grace, that is what You are giving to us.

I feel compelled to say to You, Jesus, because I can feel it in the background as you speak to Me. Many are worried about Your Words of Monday 20 December 2004 "...You wait for the Day of My Birth, My children, but I tell you that by the time it comes, millions more will be lost to Me..." and I know that within their hearts they would like to do something, if they can. Is there anything we can do?

Jesus:

I tell you that obedience to My Words is the most powerful sacrifice that anyone can give at this time. Obedience appeases My Pain and My Justice. Love and think nothing of yourself.

Patrick:

Was I right in telling Mary to paint the picture within the walls of Your House, Jesus?

Jesus:

Yes, My servant. This will bring the Graces of the prayers of My House into the Image and it will be done with My continual Blessing. No one yet knows the power of My Houses nor do they understand yet why I urge their completion. My Houses speak to all who come, even when you do not speak, My Houses speak. Respect them as you work upon them. Do it the way that I have told you and many Blessings will come from them. If it is only done in the way of the world, then what can they speak about only the world?

I still call many to My Side in these Houses of Prayer so that Love might take its place in the world once again; so that the Truth might be known.

Be obedient to My Commandments
Tuesday 21 December 2004

In these Words, My children, I give you My Love. I call you to be obe-

103

dient in these days of My Birth. If you are within My Houses, then be obedient to all that I have asked of you. If you are in the world, be obedient to My Commandments. Wherever you are, let your commitment to Me be how you love Me and your preparation for My coming. Even though I am in great loneliness at this time, let your joy in Me be complete. You will find joy in your obedience to Me. Let Me draw you to Myself in this Christmas time. Listen not to the world as it draws you ever closer to itself.

Let Me be born in you. Let My Light surround you. Let the Light of My Birth be a new time for you to begin again. Let My Words soothe you. Let My Words change you. Let My Words be recognised in you. Let your heart be open to Me. Let your heart be enriched by My Birth so that you might begin to follow Me and to serve Me the way that I have called you to.

I come to you with My Heart in My Hands as a Beggar to beg you to return to Me. I have nothing to give you but My Heart. In it is contained My Love. It is why I came; it is why I still come.

Come, little child, and be born into this Heart of Mine. It is for you. Let Me Touch you, let Me live in you. Reach out to others who do not know Me yet for, if you keep Me to yourself, what good will that do to the others who do not know Me yet?

Love Me.

Why do you hesitate?
Wednesday 22 December 2004

Patrick:
I feel You calling, Jesus, do You wish to speak?
Jesus:
Yes, My servant, I will speak. Love's Way is a good way but not many in these days choose its path. This is why I choose many to tell others of the Way that I have set out. Even among those whom I have chosen in this Way there is much reluctance to My callings. Why should this be?

I reach out in these Words, to all those whom I have chosen and indeed called, why are you afraid to be called by Me? I choose you because I wish you to do My Will. It should not be the world's business or care of the things that I have called you to do nor the way that I have called you to do it.

You, to whom I speak, you know what I have told you to do, why do you not do it? Why do you hesitate when you know that I wish it done? I have need of you.

Many of you should be out in the world bringing My Truth to those who wait for it but you prefer to sit until they come to you. This is not the way that I have called you. If I have called you to go out then you must go out. Do not take My Gifts and then sit doing nothing. The Work is hard so do not sit doing nothing.

Those whom I have called to My Houses of Prayer, why do you not come? I have spoken in your heart and you know it is I, why then do you hesitate? I have called you; come.

A few do the work of many. Read this and remember My Words:

37 "The harvest truly is plentiful, but the labourers are few.

38 Therefore pray the Lord of the harvest to send out labourers into His harvest."
Matthew 9:37-38

Many of you have taken this to mean priests only but, I tell you, the meaning of it is all whom I call. The priests who serve Me in these days are few that is why I call more workers, Prophets into My Vineyard.

Look at these Words:

1 For the kingdom of heaven is like a landowner who went out early in the morning to hire labourers for his vineyard.

2 Now when he had agreed with the labourers for a denarius a day, he sent them into his vineyard.

3 And he went out about the third hour and saw others standing idle in the marketplace,

4 and said to them, 'You also go into the vineyard, and whatever is right I will give you.' So they went.

5 Again he went out about the sixth and the ninth hour, and did likewise.

6 And about the eleventh hour he went out and found others standing idle, and said to them, 'Why have you been standing here idle all day?'

7 They said to him, 'Because no one hired us.' He said to them, 'You also go into the vineyard, and whatever is right you will receive.'

8 So when evening had come, the owner of the vineyard said to his steward, 'Call the labourers and give them their wages, beginning with the last to the first.'

9 And when those came who were hired about the eleventh hour, they each received a denarius.

10 But when the first came, they supposed that they would receive more; and they likewise received each a denarius.

11 And when they had received it, they complained against the landowner,

12 saying, 'These last men have worked only one hour, and you made them equal to us who have borne the burden and the heat of the day.'

13 But he answered one of them and said, 'Friend, I am doing you no wrong. Did you not agree with me for a denarius?

14 Take what is yours and go your way. I wish to give to this last man the same as to you.

15 Is it not lawful for me to do what I wish with my own things? Or is your eye evil because I am good?'

16 So the last will be first, and the first last. For many are called, but few chosen."
Matthew 20:1-16

Do you now see that I call many, and not just priests? There are many labourers needed in My fields. I have hired you, come now and do your work. The Master has need of you.

You shall answer to Me on Judgement Day
Wednesday 22 December 2004

Jesus:
My children, I Love you and I call you to walk in My Ways, My Footsteps. Do not listen to the false teachings of this world but only listen to the Truth that I speak within your hearts.

Listen to those teachers who teach the True Gospel Ways; the Ways that My Apostles laid down for you through My Spirit. Many heretics and blasphemers stand upon My altars and teach blasphemy to My people.

I say to you, do not listen to these for they are not Mine. Their father is the father of lies and they do his work. They change My Gospels in order to suit the sins of their lives. Do not be caught up in this, My children, for the blind can only lead the blind.

Too long have these false teachers been allowed to bring My flock in the wrong direction. Too long have they preached the gospel of self. I know you, I know you by your name and yes, you shall answer to Me on Judgement Day. Your torment shall be great for it is you yourselves that have lain the path before you. It is not too late to turn back to Me; My Forgiveness is yours if you but ask Me for it.

I Love you, My people, and I call you to follow Me in Truth. Do not allow the darkness to take you from Me. I, your Jesus, Love you and I call you back in these Words. I Love you.

Patrick:
Thank You, Jesus, I love You.

A true follower of Mine will never deny Me
Monday 27 December 2004

Jesus:
My children, I Love you. I come in these Words to call you as I have done many times in the past. I Love you, My children. My Heart Bleeds for you; My Heart longs for you to come and be part of it.

Do not allow this world to influence you any longer but turn away and know that I am with you. Know, My children, My Love for you. Know that I Died for you so that your sins would be Forgiven, so that you would have Eternal Life in My Father's Kingdom.

What more can I do for you, My children? I have Warned you of what is about to happen. I have told you the danger that you are in but you have listened to the lies of lucifer and ran with the ways of this world.

Open your eyes, My children, and look around you. Look at My Church; look at those who call themselves My shepherds, look at them change My Scripture, look at them go against the laws of My Church, look at them condemn your Holy Father (John Paul II) because he will not turn away from Me in favour of this world.

Look at your lives; how the evil one has influenced you away from Me with money. he has dangled a purse in front of you and you have accepted his favour. Where am I, children, in this world? Where am I in My own Church? I have been pushed to the fringes, out of sight for your embarrassment of Me is great. You are afraid to mention My Name in public because you know this world will not accept Me.

I can see all your deeds, My children. I know what you do, I know how you hide Me away from your friends and your fellow workers, yet you say you love Me. You deny Me in front of men. I have told you I will deny you in front of My Father for a true follower of Mine will never deny Me. A follower of Mine will believe in My existence and they will not be ashamed of Me.

Wake up, children, another year is dawning and little time have you before My Angels strike this earth with My Justice. Wake up before it is too late for your days are numbered. Soon now, you will see the evil usurper rise and he will rule over you with an iron sceptre. Yet many of you will not see nor recognise it for you have given him the sceptre to rule you with.

I Love you, My children, and I say return to Me. I say again, return for time is short.

I, your Jesus, Love you.

Patrick:
Thank You, Jesus, I love You.

Hold on to My Words
Tuesday 28 December 2004

Patrick:
Jesus, do You wish to speak?
Jesus:
My son, I Love you. I ask that you pray much for My people for very few are taking on the Words that I give to them. Rather, they are nourished by the evil of this world. Very few are willing to stop and think of Me.

My son, I Love you and I say pray, pray for My children that they will return to Me. The time of My Justice is close and there is but a remnant left. Many, many have been taken by the lies of lucifer. I ask that you hold on to My Words; nourish them within your heart so that your heart builds and becomes One with My Heart.

Please come to Me for My loneliness is great
Wednesday 29 December 2004

Jesus:
My children, I Love you. Come, delight this Heart of Mine with your love of Me. Come, children, love this lonely God so that He may know

that He is not alone.

I Love you, My children, and I ask you to spend time with Me in prayer; do not be afraid to come to Me for I long for your company. I long to hear your footsteps entering My Churches, My Houses, My Prayer Rooms.

Come, children of Mine, and love Me as I Love you. Forget about this world for a little time so that you may quench My thirst. I Love you, I Love you, I Love you. Please come to Me for My loneliness is great. I, your Jesus, await your answer. I Love you.

Patrick:

Thank You, Jesus, I love You.